UNDER GOD'S WINGS

UNDER GOD'S WINGS

Finding Daily Treasures

Phyllis (Dakota) Evanenko March

Illustrated by Lauren Karnitz

Copyright © 2019 Phyllis March. All rights reserved. Printed in the United States of America. No part of this book may be used or reproduced in any form without express written permission from the author and/or publisher except for brief quotes, approved excerpts, articles, and reviews. For information, quotes from the author, or interview requests, contact the author or publisher.

Crippled Beagle Publishing
Knoxville, Tennessee
dyer.cbpublishing@gmail. com

Scripture taken from the Amplified Bible, Copyright © 1954, 1958, 1962, 1964, 1965, 1987 by The Lockman Foundation. Used by permission. Scripture taken from the New King James Version®. Copyright © 1982 by Thomas Nelson. Used by permission. All rights reserved. Scripture quotations marked (AMP) are taken from the Amplified Bible, Copyright © 1954, 1958, 1962, 1964, 1965, 1987 by The Lockman Foundation. Used by permission." Scripture quotations taken from the Amplified® Bible Classic, Copyright © 1954, 1958, 1962, 1964, 1965, 1987, by The Lockman Foundation. Used by permission. (www.Lockman.org). Scripture quotations marked NLT are taken from the *Holy Bible*, New Living Translation, copyright © 1996, 2004, 2015 by Tyndale House Foundation. Used by permission of Tyndale House Publishers, Inc. , Carol Stream, Illinois 60188. All rights reserved. Scripture quotations marked (NIV) are taken from the Holy Bible, New International Version®, NIV®. Copyright © 1973, 1978, 1984, 2011 by Biblica, Inc. ™ Used by permission of Zondervan. All rights reserved worldwide. www. zondervan. com The "NIV" and "New International Version" are trademarks registered in the United States Patent and Trademark Office by Biblica, Inc. ™ Scripture quotations marked (TLB) are taken from The Living Bible copyright © 1971. Used by permission of Tyndale House Publishers, Inc. , Carol Stream, Illinois 60188. All rights reserved.

"Under His Wings" Lyrics: William Orcutt Cushing (1823-1902) Music: Ira David Sankey (1840-1908)

ISBN: 978-1-970037-25-8

In loving memory of Kevin March

Table of Contents

- THE BRACELET 8
- ABUNDANCE 10
- TRUST 12
- THE LAST DAY 16
- THE CONUNDRUM OF GRIEF 20
- IN LOVING MEMORY 22
- CARING FRIENDS 24
- COMMUNITY 26
- NO SPECIAL OCCASION, JUST AN OUTPOURING OF LOVE 28
- NEEDS OF OTHERS 30
- AN INNER CONVICTION 32
- BOOKS 34
- THE TREASURES OF A 12-STEP PROGRAM 38
- MASTERY OVER ONESELF 40
- BOUNDARIES 42
- MYRTLE BEACH AL-ANON CONVENTION 44
- TREASURED INSIGHT 46
- COMPLETION OF THE PAIN CAUSED BY LOSS 48
- AFTERNOON COFFEE WITH VALERIE 52
- IT'S SO MUCH MORE THAN MONEY 54
- FEDEX 56
- HOT WATER 58
- WRITING BUDS 60
- ST. GEORGE ISLAND 64
- THREE DAYS OF LA TREASURES 66
- ELEPHANT SEALS 68
- MONARCH BUTTERFLIES OF PISMO BEACH 70
- PRESERVATION HALL NEW ORLEANS 72
- HEALING FROM BROKENNESS 76
- AN AQUA BLUE TWO-WHEELER 78
- THE BLUEBIRD OF HAPPINESS 80
- RAINBOWS 82
- WOMEN'S EASTER BRUNCH 84
- EASTER CELEBRATION 86

THREE TREASURED GARDENS	88
MANNA	92
TOTAL SOLAR ECLIPSE	94
MY BROTHER PASSED AWAY	98
CANCER CHEMO BAGS	102
HEALING A BROKEN HEART	104
KEENING	106
ENERGY, PEP, AND ENDORPHINS – VITAL TREASURES	108
GOLD MEDALLION DAY	110
BREAST CANCER	114
GOD'S WORK	116
AN EMOTIONAL 24 HOURS	118
THE C-WORD	120
OPTIONS	122
ABOUT THE AUTHOR	125
ACKNOWLEDGEMENTS	127

THE BRACELET

"Under His wings I am safely abiding;
Though the night deepens and tempests are wild,
Still I can trust Him;
I know He will keep me;
He has redeemed me, and I am His child."
Verse 1, "Under His Wings"

Over the past few months I have felt God's urging to write a book about my experiences with Him. I feel very inadequate to author this book as I am not a writer but a mathematician and musician. Even though I feel angst and trepidation about my lack of words, I can choose to perceive this as a good thing since the writing will not be based on my abilities but on God speaking through me to cover my own inadequacies. God's desire is for us to be totally dependent on Him, and so I believe He will provide the words for the journey that's about to begin. The promise comes through Romans 8:26 (AMPC) which states that, "…the [Holy] Spirit comes to our aid and bears us up in our weakness" and also from 2 Corinthians 12:9 (NKJV), "My grace is sufficient for you, for My strength is made perfect in weakness."

Five and a half months after my husband Kevin passed to the other side, I received a bracelet from my dear friend Anne. This beautiful pewter bracelet has an intricately carved wing that reminds me of the song "Under His Wings," which I used to sing in church growing up. Anne was the conduit for a gift from God to remind me that I am always in His care and keeping. Not only does God keep me safe, but He also wants to shower countless treasures upon me to show His great love—constantly wooing me into a closer and more intimate spiritual relationship with Him. "God will liberally supply [my] every need according to His riches in glory in Christ Jesus." Philippians 4:19 (AMPC)

The day after I received this bracelet, I had a situation with some men who were putting up a fence between my yard and my neighbor's yard. I just happened to look outside my window that morning and saw them coming up the side of my yard and half-way onto my property. I called out to them and asked if they knew that the flags on my neighbor's yard were markers for the property line. They claimed they did not, but that they would check with the owner. A short while later I heard a knock on my door. There stood the fence men who said they'd talked to the owner and that I was correct and they would fix it. I thought to myself how lucky I was to have been home and caught the mistake before it could have become a big problem. But then I immediately had an "aha" moment that God was in charge and would take care of and protect me in every aspect of my life. I had been anxious about how I was going to handle all the things that Kevin tended to in the past; however, it became crystal clear that I could rely on a Higher Power to take care of things—even before I asked—and I did not have to worry and fret, nor try to figure things out on my own. "Do not fret *or* have any anxiety about anything, but in every circumstance *and* in everything, by prayer and petition, . . . with thanksgiving, continue to make your wants known to God." Philippians 4:6 (AMPC)

Shortly after I had this experience, I read the following verse in Isaiah 54:5 (AMPC): "For your Maker is your Husband—the Lord of hosts is His name–the Holy One of Israel is your Redeemer; the God of the whole earth He is called." Even though I had lost my earthly husband whom I dearly loved and missed, I still had a heavenly "Husband," the best provider and caretaker that I could ever need or want.

> "Under His wings, under His wings, who from His love can sever?
> Under His wings my soul shall abide, safely abide forever."
> Chorus from "Under His Wings"

ABUNDANCE

"I'm drinking from my saucer 'cause my cup has overflowed."
—John Paul Moore

Some years ago I heard on the radio this song sung by Michael Combs. Based on the poem by John Paul Moore, the lyrics and music left a huge impression on me since for years I had practiced "poverty consciousness-thinking" in most, if not all, areas of my life. This song suggested something quite the opposite. Financial insecurity topped the list of my apprehensions. I was fear driven and felt that my cup was empty, not half empty nor half full, but *completely* empty. This song presented a whole new concept to me—one in which my cup was so full that it was overflowing into my saucer. Wow! That was a huge paradigm shift, so I decided to practice a new thought process of financial abundance using the words of this song as my mantra. Over the years as I daily kept the concept ever before me, something began to happen in my subconscious mind. I started to believe it and at some point I realized that I was no longer fearful about money issues. In fact, fear of economic insecurity had left me and had been replaced with prosperity consciousness.

During this undertaking, I learned the importance of using two important principles described by Deepak Chopra in *The Seven Spiritual Laws of Success*: "The Law of Intention and Desire" and "The Law of Least Effort." As a third principle, I coined "The Law of Substitution" to replace my negative self-talk. God, as well as these powerful ideas, assisted in the effort to change my perceptions from fear and poverty to love and prosperity. This technique worked and it created in me a desire to apply the process to other areas of personal concern to produce a richer, fuller life.

In the process, I have come to realize that the abundant life is not so much about health and wealth but about having an abundance of reliance on and faith in God. Primarily, I am seeking a bounty of experiences with God that will illumine His existence as well as His great love for me. Jesus, in John 10:10 (NKJV), says "I have come that they may have life, and that they may have it more abundantly." Life is a sequence of physical, mental, and spiritual experiences that make up the existence of an individual and Jesus tells us that He wants us to have life—all aspects of it—more abundantly.

My part in this life's journey is to open myself to Spirit through daily prayer and meditation. God's part is to fill that opening with His treasures found in Galatians 5:22-23 (the fruit of the Spirit—love, joy, peace, patience, kindness, goodness, faithfulness, gentleness, and self-control), all amply manifested, so that I may know the width, height, and depth of Christ's love and be filled with all the fullness of God, as promised in Eph 3:18-19.

"I thank God for all His blessings on me and the mercy He's bestowed.
I'm drinking from my saucer cause my cup has overflowed."
—John Paul Moore

TRUST

"Trust in the Lord with all your heart,
And lean not on your own understanding . . . ."
Proverbs 3:5 (NKJV)

My new word for the year is *trust*. For the past five or six years, God has impressed upon me a word to focus on each year. *Grace* was one such word, another time it was *fun* (I actually had to use *fun* two years in a row because I needed to practice it longer), last year it was *patience*, and now the word is *trust*. For the first two weeks of this year, I actually thought I had three words: *community, contribution,* and *compassion*, and though I also need to work on them, my main focus will be on *trust*. I received my word this morning as I read the January 4th page of the book *Jesus Calling* by Sarah Young." I want you to learn a new habit. Try saying, 'I trust You, Jesus. '" I knew that word was being delivered directly to me as it fits right in with my greatest need and desire—to "know" on a heart-felt level that God exists and desires a personal relationship with me.

For a number of years I prayed for God to show me that He is real. Then the afternoon that Kevin was passing, as I read to him from his Bible highlighted with all of the promises of God and His grace, I realized that God was speaking directly to me. My word for last year—*patience*—and my desire to know that God is real were interwoven and connected through the word *trust*. Romans 5:2-5 (NLT) states we can:

> *. . . confidently and joyfully look forward to actually becoming all that God has had in mind for us to be. We can rejoice, too, when we run into problems and trials, for we know that they are good for us—they help us learn to be patient. And patience develops strength of character in us and helps us trust God more each time we use it until finally our hope and faith are strong and steady. Then, when that happens, we are able to hold our heads high no matter happens and know that all is well, for we know how dearly God loves us, and we feel this warm love everywhere within us . . . .*

It blew my mind when I read those verses. They were a huge gift from God as Kevin was about to make his transition. The verses proclaimed that if I practiced patience, my trust in God would be strengthened, and then, finally, I would truly believe. I had always been like a reed blowing in the wind in regard to His existence, and whichever way the wind blew, that's the direction I leaned. But God's wonderful promise showed me a way out of this unsteadiness and uncertainty. The timing could not have been more perfect; I needed something concrete to hold onto since Kevin was being taken to another realm and I was in deep mourning, already experiencing the tremendous loss of my partner and soulmate. Two hours later Kevin peacefully passed, and I could rest assured that, in time, I would have an inner conviction that God exists and Kevin is with Him.

> "Trust in the Lord with all your heart,
> And lean not on your own understanding;
> In all your ways acknowledge Him,
> And He shall direct your paths."
> Proverbs 3:5-6 (NKJV)

"Where there is ruin, there is hope for treasure."
—Rumi

THE LAST DAY

> "For our present troubles are small and won't last very long. Yet they produce for us a glory that vastly outweighs them and will last forever!!" 2 Corinthians 4:17 (NLT)

When I woke up the morning of July 15, little did I know that Kevin would be passing quickly from this world. Instinctively, I knew that I needed to call someone to help me get a handle on things that seemed to be spiraling out of control. I didn't know what to do and didn't know that this would be Kevin's last day. I called my friend Lyle, not sure why she came to mind that morning, but sometime later I knew that God had planned it that way. Her father had passed away from cancer a few years before, and hospice had been called in to assist with his end of life care. Shortly, she appeared at my door and when she saw Kevin sprawled out on the bed and unresponsive, she said hospice needed to be called in immediately. I phoned the oncologist's office where Kevin was promptly set up with Amedisys Hospice in Sweetwater. As we waited for the nurse to arrive, Lyle showed me how to swab Kevin's dry lips with water to make him feel more comfortable as well as exactly where the meds should be placed in his mouth.

About an hour later, a male hospice nurse came over and upon examining Kevin estimated that he had fewer than 72 hours left. I was shocked! It all seemed so surreal and was happening way too fast. But, I was beyond grateful for my friend Lyle, who was there and took copious notes as the nurse described the events that would be forthcoming. The nurse ordered morphine to be immediately delivered to the house and prescribed the dosage that was strong enough to keep Kevin's pain at bay. After everything was in order, the nurse and my friend left, as I wanted to spend some time alone with Kevin, reading to him from his Bible.

In the afternoon, a hospice social worker came over, looked in on Kevin, and said that he had fewer than 48 hours. I was distraught upon hearing the shortened number of hours. We talked a bit and I told her that Kevin wanted to donate his organs to people in need, but they were in such bad shape she suggested that I instead donate his body to MedCure for medical research. I knew that's exactly what Kevin would have wanted and would have been thrilled to know that a free cremation would be thrown in once the research was concluded. After all the papers were signed, I was alone once again with Kevin.

I continued to read to him from his Bible, not knowing if he could hear. Understanding that hearing was the last thing to go before death, I presumed he was listening. My friend Kathy had shared the following verse with me that beautifully summed up Kevin's life: 2 Timothy 4:7 (NIV), "I have fought the good fight, I have finished the race, I have kept the faith." I read it numerous times to him throughout the afternoon and wanted him to know that it was okay to make his transition. In fact, I encouraged him to go. I kept reminding him that God and all the angels, as well as his loved ones who had already passed, were waiting to welcome him home. I also repeatedly read the following poem from a hospice booklet titled *Gone From My Sight: The Dying Experience* and distributed by Barbara Karnes:

Gone From My Sight
by Henry Van Dyke (also credited to Rev. Luther F. Beecher)

I am standing upon the seashore. A ship at my side spreads her white sails to the morning breeze and starts for the blue ocean. She is an object of beauty and strength. I stand and watch her until at length she hangs like a speck of white cloud just where the sea and sky come to mingle with each other. Then someone at my side says: "There, she is gone!"
"Gone where?"
Gone from my sight. That is all. She is just as large in mast and hull and spar as she was when she left my side and she is just as able to bear the load of living freight to her destined port. Her diminished size is in me, not in her. And just at the moment when someone at my side says: "There, she is gone!" There are other eyes watching her coming, and other voices ready to take up the glad shout: "Here she comes!"
And that is dying…

At about 7:40 p. m., Kevin's breathing became more labored, and I was concerned that he might be in pain. So, I stepped into an adjacent room and called a hospice nurse who told me to increase his morphine dosage. After I hung up, I stepped into the kitchen to prepare the meds and a few minutes later returned to Kevin with the syringe. During the few minutes that I was gone, Kevin had passed away. I was heart-broken as I wanted to be present when he died. But, I have been reassured by others that sometimes a person who is dying will wait until their loved one is out of the room to take his or her last breath. And that is how it happened at 7:45 p.m. It was not 72, nor 48, but only eight hours from when hospice had first arrived. Even though it was much shorter than had been anticipated, it was a treasure to be able to assist my husband at the end of his earthly journey. God's promise was true indeed.

> ". . . The troubles will soon be over,
> but the joys to come will last forever."
> 2 Corinthians 4:18 (TLB)

*All spiritual warriors have a broken heart—
alas, must have a broken heart—
because it is only through the break
that the wonder and mysteries of life can enter us.*
—Tibetan myth

THE CONUNDRUM OF GRIEF

"Jesus wept." John 11:35

It's hard to believe that just this morning I was praising God and thanking Him for the many daily treasures bestowed upon me, yet by evening I was in the pit of deep despair and profound despondency. Over the last couple of weeks I was doing quite well, I thought, being in God's will and writing about His marvelous works, but tonight I can't stop crying and can't even begin to fathom His plan. I miss Kevin so much and want to share the events and happenings in my life with him. I don't understand how God could take my soulmate and leave me behind. Couldn't He have taken us both at the same time?

I sympathize with Job. In Chapter 3, Verse 1 (NLT), he "opened his mouth and cursed the day of his birth." I, too, at times, wish I'd never been born so that I wouldn't have to experience this horrendous heartbreak and sorrow. However, the readings of Job point to another view and perspective. Though Job didn't understand why everything was taken from him, he continued to pray and put his faith and trust in God. In Job 19:25 (NKJV) he professed, "For I know *that* my Redeemer lives, and He shall stand at last on the earth."

I, too, like Job, am discovering that when pain and agony wash over me, I can call on God to strengthen and help me. He always does in some form or another. And since my greatest hope and desire is to know that God is real, my trials and tribulations are but channels my Higher Power uses to further that aim. I am being led to more wisdom and greater understanding and look forward to the day when I can firmly declare, "I have heard of You by the hearing of the ear, but now my [spiritual] eye sees you." Job 42:5 (NKJV)

I can rest reassured that God understands all of my emotions, especially the grief and mourning that threaten to overcome me from time to time, because His Spirit experienced it. The shortest verse in the Bible, but I believe one with the greatest emotional impact, reveals that the Holy Spirit can relate to our grief and sorrow because He also felt great pain in the death of His friend Lazarus.

"Jesus wept." John 11:35

IN LOVING MEMORY

"If tears could build a stairway, and memories build a lane,
I'd walk right up to heaven and bring you home again."
—author unknown

My thoughtful, caring friend, Kelly, gave me a beautiful pewter pendant with the above quote etched on it in loving memory of Kevin. I cannot begin to express the magnitude and depth of meaning these types of gifts have been for me. I treasure this pendant greatly as I wear it tied on a red ribbon encircled around my neck. It is a reminder that though Kevin is not physically here, he is with me in my heart.

I wish that I could bring Kevin home, again. So many times over the past six years I brought him home—from hospitals, emergency rooms, and doctors' offices. Oh, to be able to do it one more time—to share with him and connect soul-to-soul, to wipe his brow and to offer him words of encouragement and hope. He was the love of my life and it all went way too fast. I would like an extension, please.

Kevin thought he had two months left. I let myself believe that, too, even though the oncologist said he had only a few days. I didn't want to believe it; I wanted so badly to believe Kevin even though it wasn't true. When I told Kevin the doctor's pronouncement, he pooh-poohed it and said not to believe him—that the doctor didn't know what he was talking about. Kevin had no idea that two days later he would be gone, nor did I. Yet, I believe it was for the best even though I didn't like it. According to God's plan those two days were better than two months." And we know that all things work together for good . . . ." Rom 8:28 (NKJV)

It is with joy in my heart that I can thank God for the last number of years that I did have with Kevin and for the many blessings that were continually bestowed on us as we journeyed together along this human/spiritual path.

"I will praise *You*, O Lord, with my whole heart; I will tell of all Your marvelous works." Psalm 9:1 (NKJV)

CARING FRIENDS

> "I will praise You, O Lord, with my whole heart;
> I will show forth all Your marvelous works *and* wonderful deeds!"
> Psalm 9:1 (AMPC)

Every morning over the past year, Kevin and I would head to McDonald's and arrive there by 9:00 a.m. for a breakfast of eggs and egg whites, a Diet Coke, and coffee. It became a treasured ritual for us to spend time talking and doing crossword and acrostic puzzles as we started each new day. Our dear friend Macy provided us with many a gift card to demonstrate her wish to be there for us as Kevin traveled a formidable cancer journey. We thought of her each time we used a card and were grateful to have her there in spirit as we enjoyed our meals. Her beneficence, as well as the kindheartedness of others, embodied the verse, "A friend loves at all times." Proverbs 17:17 (NIV)

We were also grateful for meals that Nancy, Kimberly, Denise, and Jamie lovingly brought over. The food provided much needed sustenance and nourishment to help us endure the most challenging of times. There is nothing like a delicious hot meal to counteract the effects of chemo and strong medication.

Both Kevin and I felt that caring friends are one of life's most valuable gifts, and it was through their goodness and loving kindness that we were able to not only survive, but to also move forward after Kevin was diagnosed with stage IV large diffuse B-cell lymphoma. It was a colossal shock, a titanic trauma, a jolt of paralysis to our psyches to hear the crushing news, and we needed a Higher Power to direct our path. We also needed loving friends to hold and comfort us in our hour of need.

After making three automobile trips in four months' time to MD Anderson in Houston, Texas, to try to set up a treatment plan for Kevin, we relied on a caring God to see us through the enormous challenge. We weren't let down; God's provision for us was through friends with skin on. The cards, phone calls, texts, emails, meals, and gifts that we received helped and encouraged us to keep on keeping on. Friends regularly prayed for our stamina and well-being. Our community of loved ones carried out Galatians 6:2 (NKJV), "Bear one another's burdens, and so fulfill the law of Christ." They helped us feel less alone, which fortified us with renewed strength and endurance.

"I will praise You, O Lord, among the peoples;
I will sing to You among the nations." Psalm 57:9 (NKJV)

COMMUNITY

"Each of you should look not only to your own interest, but also to the interests of others." Philippians 2:4 (NIV)

Because our community of loved ones and friends was always thinking of us, encouraging us, and helping us, Kevin's transition was made much easier. The last week of his life he spent two days in the hospital before coming back home. While we were at the hospital, a number of friends stopped by to see him—Kimberly and Tom, Kathy and Jim, Maureen, and Nancy—and that helped a great deal to relieve his concerns about me and to pass in peace a few days later. Kevin had a great deal of anxiety that I would have a difficult time after he departed, and since his nature was to think about others, he, of course, was worried about how I would fare. He told Nancy he could see that I had a lot of friends who would support and tend to me after he was gone, and that sustained him.

The home visits from Nancy and Tim, Marsha and Don, Brian and Marce, Shondra and Jim, as well as many others, were a joyous time of fellowship and laughter that cheered and nurtured Kevin. In Romans 1:12 the Bible says we should be mutually strengthened, encouraged, and comforted by each other's faith, and we were, indeed.

The phone calls from Monica, Macy, Amy, and a host of others who regularly checked on us were a welcome interlude in the day-to-day hardship and affliction that were Kevin's lot as he moved along his path. It helped so much to know that others were thinking of us and praying for our welfare. Verse 1Thessalonians. 5:14 (NLT), ". . . Take tender care of those who are weak . . . ." was fulfilled in so many wonderful ways by our dear loved ones. Without that tender care it would have been much harder to walk this journey.

"Because of your prayers and the help the Holy Spirit gives me, all of this will turn out for good." Philippians 1:19 (NLV)

NO SPECIAL OCCASION, JUST AN OUTPOURING OF LOVE

"May the Lord make your love increase and overflow for each other and for everyone else . . . ." 1 Thessalonians 3:12 (NIV)

At a coffee gathering yesterday, two of my friends gave me a beautiful offering of their love. Since it was not a special occasion, it made the gifts even more memorable.

My friend Kimberly had previously taken photographs of two of my paintings which I had created on my trip to California with friend Marsha, at a five-day acrylic painting workshop with artist Bob Burridge. The first painting was of a heart with red background and a string coming out of the bottom, as if it were a heart-shaped balloon sailing in the sky. A brown ladder reaches up to its base and invites entry into this heart for those desiring to make the climb.

Kimberly designed a card with this heart-shaped painting on the front; on the back she placed a photo of my wing bracelet featured on top of my baby grand piano keys—two favorite possessions of mine—with the caption: "Original painting by Phyllis March." By preparing this, she cleverly turned my art into her art and devised a very functional, personalized greeting card in the process. In fact, twenty of these cards were printed by Shutterfly, the printing vendor.

Then Kimberly took my second painting of a blue vase with salmon-colored flowers and had a tiny replica embedded on refrigerator magnets, which I proudly put on display. My art teacher said this vase-with-flowers painting looked like a Matisse. I think he was just being overly enthusiastic and said that to bolster me up, as well as to keep me coming to class. I am beyond grateful to Kimberly for these two wonderful treasures.

My friend Kelly who knows what it's like to walk the cancer journey, having had it herself and been cured, gave me a beautiful sea green box that has a ceramic ivory heart on top with the following inscription: "Friends are like stars. You don't have to see them to know they are there." Inside the box is a lovely ceramic ivory cup with the same inscription on the front. Kelly is one of those kinds of friends, a star, and Kevin and I were blessed greatly by her generous and charitable spirit. She gives out comfort/care bags to folks who have cancer and lovingly attends to many friends and acquaintances who have this devastating illness. She charitably prepares these tote bags and includes many items patients need that are usually not provided by cancer centers and hospitals. Kelly made one such care bag for my husband, and he was delighted and grateful to receive from her bountiful supply. It was one of his last treasures.

"Therefore comfort *and* encourage one another with these words."
1 Thessalonians 4:18 (AMPC)

NEEDS OF OTHERS

"When God's children are in need, you be the one to help them out."
Romans 12:13 (TLB)

Though Kevin and I never had children of our own, we had a great desire to help and provide for their needs. When Kevin's niece Lori and her husband Rob adopted four foster children, we helped out financially with some of the "extras" that brought an added degree of happiness to the children's lives. Contributing to vacations and buying toys brightened our lives immeasurably, as much as we hope it did theirs. We especially enjoyed purchasing toys with lights and sounds for their child with Down syndrome who played with the toys for hours on end in great joyful delight. But our gifts to the children pale in comparison to the stable, devoted, and loving home that Rob and Lori provide for them. These special angels share what they have with others and are an immense blessing to all who know them.

At Christmastime each year, we attended the Toys for Tots concert and took new toys to be given away to needy children. We had made it known to all of our friends and loved ones that we would prefer them contribute to the needs of others, instead of giving to us because doing for others gave us so much pleasure and our own cups were overflowing. "It is more blessed to give than to receive." Acts 20:35 (NIV)

Our friends Macy and Kimberly honored that request in two very special ways. When Kevin would go for chemo treatment, it broke our hearts to see bald-headed, young children in pain with IVs dripping in their arms and being pushed around the hospital in wheelchairs by their worried, anxious, and distraught parents. After Kevin passed away, my friend Macy surprised me with a donation in honor and memory of Kevin to St. Jude's Children's Hospital for research in the treatment of children's cancers. She also made a contribution in my name. Kevin would have been as pleased as I was to know that these gifts would contribute to the well-being and, someday, hopefully soon, eradication of cancer in children.

Kimberly also made a contribution in Kevin's honor to Water.org, which helps bring safe water to people in need around the world. The card I received from the company stated: "May this gift bring you happiness, as it brings women hope, children health, and communities a future," and also included the following statement by Mother Teresa: "It's not how much we give but how much love we put into giving." I was thrilled that these lifesaving treasures in Kevin's name would be blessing others in a multitude of ways through the generosity and kindness of our dear friends.

"Don't just pretend to love others. Really love them."
Romans 12:9 (NLT)

AN INNER CONVICTION

> "And so I tell you, keep on asking, and you will receive what you ask for. Keep on seeking, and you will find. Keep on knocking, and the door will be opened to you." Luke 11:9 (NLT)

The above verse must be a very important one, because it is immediately repeated in Luke 11:10. I believe it is the key to manifest the longing in my heart, which is to have a deeply rewarding, intimate relationship with a Higher Power. The importance of asking, seeking, and persevering in the attempt to have this personal connection cannot be overstated. I told my friends over the past year about how badly I wanted to "know" that God really exists and wasn't just a figment of the imagination. It became the most important need in my life, and I had a burning desire to know Him on a spiritual level. Deuteronomy 4:29 (NIV) encouraged me that my hunger would be granted. "But if from there you seek the LORD your God, you will find him if you seek him with all your heart and with all your soul."

    Growing up, I weekly went to church and developed a belief in God on an intellectual basis, but I didn't really have Him in my heart. I had yearned for and prayed that my inner experience would match up with my outward belief and that I could perceive this love of His that surpasses all knowledge and understanding. From the promise in Ephesians 3:16 (NIV), I was most hopeful that it could be attained: "...out of his glorious riches he may strengthen you with power thorough his Spirit in your inner being."

    According to Franciscan Priest Richard Rohr, "All spiritual traditions at their mature levels agree that such a movement is possible, desirable, and even available to everyone." And I had an unquenchable thirst to move from my belief system to an actual inner experience.

    Every day, God fulfills His promises and brings me closer to the desires of my heart. The more I acknowledge His bountiful gifts, and am appreciative and thankful for His many treasures, the more there seem to be. He opens my eyes ever wider and reveals His goodness and glory. In writing about these experiences and sharing about His tremendous love and care, there is a stirring in my own soul and a strengthening of my trust in and closeness to Him. As I ask, seek, and persevere, God is ever preparing me for a closer and closer soul-walk with Him, and I am grateful.

> "Everyone who asks, receives; all who seek, find;
> and the door is opened to everyone who knocks."
> Luke 11:10 (TLB)

BOOKS

> "If any of you lacks wisdom, let him ask of God, who gives to all liberally and without reproach, and it will be given to him."
> James 1:5 (NKJV)

I am like a kid at Christmas when I get a new book. I can hardly wait to open the pages and see what's inside. There is often a great deal of wisdom that can be found between its covers. Even though I'm a slow reader, I am always anxious to get started on the journey the book will take me on because I know there will be many treasures I will gather along the way.

For example, my greatest desire, to "know God" on an emotional, spiritual level and not just intellectually, has been a longing of mine since I was a kid. Though I consciously didn't know it at the time, I gradually came to the awareness that I wanted a solid level of conviction—a strong belief that there is a God who deeply cares about all of us. Then this morning I read in Anne Lamott's book *Help, Thanks, Wow* about Pedro Arrupe, a devout man of God, elected head of the Jesuits in 1965, who wrote in his journal: "More than ever I find myself in the hands of God. This is what I have wanted all my life, from my youth. But now there is a difference. The initiative is entirely with God. It is indeed a profound spiritual experience to know and feel myself to be totally in God's hands."

It gives me hope that if Arrupe's desire was realized, then mine can be, too. I just have to keep asking my Higher Power for patience and trust, and the faith to perceive that this desire has already been fulfilled; I just haven't recognized it, yet.

> "I know that You can do everything . . . ." Job 42:2 (NKJV)

I love the synchronicity of life. Had it not been for a friend who gave me *Bird by Bird*, another of Lamott's books, I would not have gone to my bookcase to see if I had anything else by her. And sure enough, there was *Help, Thanks, Wow* which I had purchased years ago, then put on the shelf where it was just waiting for a re-read at this particular point in time. Every time I take a second look at a treasured book more wisdom and insight are extended to me through one of God's many channels.

Recently, I read that it's not about the destination, but about the journey. In my eagerness to have this kind of spiritual experience, right now, I don't want to miss out on all of the other treasures along the way.

> "The fear of the Lord is the beginning of wisdom,
> And the knowledge of the Holy One is understanding."
> Proverbs 9:10 (NIV)

*All buried seeds
crack open in the dark
the instant they surrender
to a process they can't see.*
—Mark Nepo

THE TREASURES OF A 12-STEP PROGRAM

"Show me Your ways, O Lord; teach me Your paths."
Psalm 25:4 (NKJV)

Last night I attended a speaker meeting at Park 40 where my friend Maureen told her story. It was very insightful, as well as entertaining, and since I love to laugh and try to find the humor in things, she didn't disappoint. Because Maureen has been through some hard, tough stuff in her life, she is adept at empathizing with others and putting them at ease. She spoke from the heart about her life and we were all able to cry, laugh, and connect with her as she courageously recalled her past experiences.

Prior to the meeting Maureen, Macy (another friend), and I met at the Cracker Barrel for dinner. When I got there, I noticed that my space at the table already had something on it. As I looked more closely, I saw that it was a huge piece of Reese's cheesecake which Macy had picked up for me at the Cheesecake Factory. I was surprised and amazed, and also very happy! Macy heard me when I had told her once, a few weeks ago, that I had gone to the Cheesecake Factory in California twice because I loved their Reese's cheesecake. Friends who listen and "hear" me are one of the many gifts of the 12-step program, and Macy has fine-tuned her listening skills to not only hear what I'm saying but also to act on what she's heard. I really appreciate her ability to demonstrate that kind of caring, especially when it comes to desserts!

Please note that my friends asked that I share their real names. Close, meaningful relationships are a treasured part of the program, but there are also many other gifts. The slogans, for example, provide brief, succinct tips to deal with stressful and/or uncomfortable situations. **"One Day at a Time"** is a good reminder to stay in the present day, hour, or moment to deal with the issues at hand. **"HALT"** prompts me to stop and take care of myself when I am **H**ungry, **A**ngry, **L**onely, or **T**ired. **"Let Go and Let God"** is a good suggestion when I think I have to figure some problem out on my own. **"Live and Let Live"** helps keep me from getting on other people's roller coasters and going up and down with their thoughts and feelings. If I keep my nose out of their business, they can choose how they want to live their lives without my unwarranted and unsolicited advice.

"Detach" says **D**on't **E**ven **T**hink **A**bout **C**hanging **H**im/**H**er. It's hard enough to change myself; it's insane to think I could change someone else but does that stop me from trying?! And then there is **"Fear"** which could mean either **F**ace **E**verything **A**nd **R**ecover or **F**orgot **E**verything's **A**ll **R**ight. Maybe the most destructive word is **"Shame,"** **S**hould **H**ave **A**lready **M**astered **E**verything. My friend Macy has been a great source of comfort for me when I go into "shaming and beating myself up" mode. When I say, "I should have known better," she counters by saying, "How could you have known?" Since there is so much that I don't know, it is a very comforting response. Life is all about trial-and-error, learning, practicing, accepting, and forgiving myself and others.

These slogans and others, plus the 12-Steps, 12-Traditions, 12-Concepts, and 12-Step literature, as well as the opportunities to hear the honest stories from other people in the program, are a treasure trove of resources that can contribute to the growth and healing of individuals who want to pursue a healthier way of being. The goal, to experience more peace and serenity, joy, and happiness in life, can be attained by working the program.

> "My inner self thirsts for God, for the living God."
> Psalm 42:2 (AMPC)

MASTERY OVER ONESELF

"And the Lord restored Job's losses when he prayed for his friends. Indeed the Lord gave Job twice as much as he had before."
Job 42:10 (NKJV)

I had an opportunity to meet with my treasured friend Brenda today. She wrote a book, *Silent Scars*, about her experiences of being married for 30 years to Gary, a Vietnam veteran with post-traumatic stress disorder (PTSD.) After the war, she said Gary would walk the perimeter of their land at night to make sure they were safe, just like he did in Vietnam. He buried his experiences in "Nam" deep within himself but was fearful and on edge, and it would take over twenty years for the family to finally get some help. Sadly, by then a lot of water had already gone over the dam.

It seems that the whole family was affected by Gary's enlistment in the war, and there would be silent scars on all of them for the rest of their lives. Brenda has her own form of PSTD in having lived through all those years of her husband's flashbacks and nightmares. "I did not enlist in a war, but looking back it seemed like I was drafted, too," she told me. Even though they struggled and tried hard to overcome the after-effects of war, their marriage did not survive; however, Brenda's spirit is bright. She has a strong faith and helps others who are going through great losses and huge upsets. I am so blessed to have her in my life.

This afternoon Brenda and I went with some friends to see the movie *A United Kingdom*, which is about the marriage of a white British woman to a black man named Seretse Khama, who was schooled in England in preparation to become king of Botswana, Africa. The movie is based on a true story that took place in the '50s and the struggles and prejudices that this interracial couple endured and overcame. In the movie, Seretse quotes Greek philosopher Epictetus, saying, "No man is free who is not master of himself." This sentence speaks to me about John 8:32 (TLB): ". . . and you will know the truth, and the truth will set you free." With God's help, the Truth sets us free to master those things like addictions, obsessions, delusions, and negative self-talk that keep us chained up and imprisoned in our minds.

I think of my friend Brenda and how hard she works with her Higher Power to transform her losses into blessings. Her favorite song is the Michael Combs version of "Drinking from My Saucer." Her cup has overflowed! She is freeing herself from the gut-wrenching experiences she has endured and is replacing them with the Truth that an abundance of God's goodness is overflowing in her life. Now that's self-mastery and freedom at its best.

> "Now the Lord blessed the latter days of Job more than his beginning." Job 42:12 (NKJV)

BOUNDARIES

"Let us live and conduct ourselves honorably and becomingly as in the [open light] of day." Romans 13:13 (AMPC)

There were no boundaries when I was growing up; instead there was an enmeshment with my mother which was emotionally stifling, strangling, suffocating, and pervasive. Consequently, today I have difficulty in setting boundaries with others because I don't know what I need for my own safety and protection. Since boundaries are a necessary ingredient for high self-esteem and a prerequisite for having healthy relationships with others, I am desirous to discover more about this protective tool.

It is heartening to realize that my Higher Power respects boundaries and doesn't just enter in without asking, as evidenced in Revelations 3:20 (NKJV): "Behold, I stand at the door and knock. If anyone hears My voice and opens the door, I will come in to him and dine with him, and he with Me." This verse is a treasured revelation for me, illustrating the respect God has for boundaries and for allowing us freedom of choice.

Because I have difficulty in this area, I can over-step my bounds with others and deem the boundaries they should establish. I have the mistaken idea that if they just did such and such, then I would feel safe and secure. But that's interfering with their lives and their freedom of choice, which I loathe doing. It can be very confusing because sometimes I can't discern whether or not someone is doing something that is hurting me or if I'm doing something potentially damaging.

What I think I know about boundaries is that they can be flexible; they're not the same as putting up walls; I can change my mind, if needed, and they are for my protection and safety. I think it's important for me to realize that I'm just at the beginning of trying to learn something new and that I'm going to be making a lot of mistakes. Even though this process looks pretty messy from my standpoint, as long as I keep on trying, I will eventually become more accomplished with grace and dignity. And I won't feel like a newborn calf trying to stand up.

I'm not alone in this challenging problem. Samson, too, had boundary issues as noted in the book of Judges. He started out as a Biblical leader with healthy boundaries which were soon worn down. Samson's wife prodded him to tell her the answer to a riddle he had posed to the Philistines, and when he didn't, she tearfully accused him of not loving her enough until he finally caved in to her demand and told her. She in turn revealed the answer to his enemies. But, did Samson learn from his mistake (boundary lesson) the first time? No! He did have another opportunity to try again, just as I believe we all get multiple opportunities to learn lessons that are designed for our individual growth on life's journey.

The next situation for Samson to practice better boundaries was when he met Delilah, who tried to entice him to reveal the source of his power and great strength. Though he kept his secret for a while, he eventually became entranced and gave her the explanation (his long hair), which unfortunately led to his demise. The importance of having healthy boundaries cannot be over-emphasized in this situation, as well as in any relationship. Manipulation can be used to control another, and when the evidence points to not being respected, loved, and supported, it is time to consider the reason for staying—especially when it appears that one will be destroyed if one remains. Establishing and maintaining healthy boundaries is crucial to having fulfilling, flourishing relationships that last.

Counselor and author John Bradshaw describes his image of ideal relationships as ". . . people making music together. Each plays his own instrument and uses his own unique skills, but they play the same song. Each is whole and complete. Each is independent and committed." And I'd also like to include in that description that each person is willing to respect and exercise healthy boundaries with the another.

> ". . . Work out your own salvation . . . for it is God who works in you both to will and to do for His good pleasure."
> Philippians 2:12, 13 (NKJV)

MYRTLE BEACH AL-ANON CONVENTION

"Be strong and of good courage . . . for the Lord your God, He is the One who goes with you. He will not leave you nor forsake you."
Deut. 31:6 (NKJV)

It was a treasure to be able to attend the Al-Anon Convention at Myrtle Beach, South Carolina, this year with seven other awesome women from my area, seekers who wish to grow and lead a more spirit-filled life. With so many wonderful sessions and speaker meetings available, it was a huge smorgasbord of opportunities from which to pick and choose those subjects that individually resonated with each of us. Because some of the topics we wished to attend were in the same time slot, we made sure members of our group covered all of those pertinent discussions, and later we shared the key points and essential details. We were hungry for suggestions and tips in how to better conduct ourselves so we could experience more peace and serenity in our relationships. In other words, we wanted the Serenity Prayer, written by theologian Reinhold Niebuhr, to be more consistently demonstrated in our lives.

God grant me the serenity to accept the things I cannot change,
Courage to change the things I can,
And wisdom to know the difference.

For example, one seminar was titled "Courage to Trust Myself and My Decisions," which is right on topic with the Serenity Prayer. How can I have the courage to change the things I can if I don't first have the courage to trust myself and my decisions?! One of the things I heard is that if I "pause" instead of going forward at breakneck speed into a situation, and I humbly wait for God's direction for the next step to take, then the outcome will be the most beneficial for all concerned. Lesson 47 of *The Course in Miracles* states that "God is the strength in which I trust and that only God can resolve situations in such a way that only good can come of it." So, if I desire the best solution, then it would behoove me to "take a break" from my mind and ask God to make His plan known and understood. Secondly, I need to ask for courage, which our Higher Power will abundantly provide. So, how can one best respond to the following Yogi Berra quote? "When you come to a fork in the road, take it." The answer is to pause to gain discernment and then ask for courage to go down the particular path that's shown.

As I learn to trust, the more I practice this two-step process, I begin to see that confusion is a gift that keeps me from acting unwisely and prematurely. I will be divinely led when it's time to act and make a decision when my head, heart, and gut are all lined up. I don't have to stew and worry and fret about it being the wrong decision or that I somehow misinterpreted God's guidance. I don't need to judge my decisions, but at times, some adaptions may need to be made. Sometimes big and major adjustments are necessary, but that's okay if I allow God to use those adjustments as a learning, teachable moments for me. Then, as I grow in confidence through this process, I gain wisdom to discern the things that I can and cannot change and demonstrate the courage and acceptance to appropriately do so.

> "Trust in the LORD with all your heart and lean not on your own understanding; in all your ways submit to him, and he will make your paths straight. Do not be wise in your own eyes." Proverbs 3:5-7 (NIV)

TREASURED INSIGHT

"Unto You, O Lord, do I bring my life. O my God, I trust, lean on, rely on, *and* am confident in You. Let me not be put to shame *or* [my hope in You] be disappointed . . . ." Psalm 25:1-2 (AMPC)

I had a shame attack the other day and there is nothing that psychologically can hurt me more than that. It is like having an anxiety attack, a panic attack, and a fear attack all rolled into one. I did not initially know what was happening to me, except that the emotional pain was extremely intense and severe. After journaling, praying, reading Al-Anon literature, and sharing my pain and feelings with a trusted friend (things suggested in the 12-Step Program to become more peaceful and serene), I recognized the old symptoms/feelings of a shame attack that I hadn't experienced in a long time (years, in fact). I was beating myself up over a decision I had made and was worried I had made the wrong choice.

The trait of perfectionism—to make the perfect, right decision at all times—was passed on to me from my mother who always agonized over decision-making situations, so fearful that she'd make the wrong choice. For example, if she were buying a dress, it would be very hard for her to decide (hypothetically), between the red one and the blue one, and when she finally did make a decision, it was almost always the wrong one, and she would be unhappy and dissatisfied. This represents perfectionism at its finest.

I, too, used to be distressed when it came time to make a decision, but with practice and the help of program tools, I have gotten much better. Now, after an analysis of the facts, I can usually make a timely decision that I'm comfortable with in most situations, but I still find it a challenge in the area of relationships. And that's what my shame attack was all about—a relationship issue. I felt I had made a wrong choice and that I should have known better.

Fortunately, I received a profound insight from my Higher Power and became heart-consciously aware that, since I based my decision on the information I had at the time, it was the best I could do. When more information became available, as it did, I was able to adapt and make a different choice based on new knowledge and facts I had obtained. I heard a woman share in a recovery meeting that there are no right or wrong decisions, but there might need to be some adjustments along the way, perhaps some major adjustments. This is a much kinder, gentler way of looking at this process, compared to agonizing over the "perfect" decision.

In regard to feeling that I should have known better with the first choice I had made, the reading in *Courage to Change* for October 18 states, "I may not recognize it right now, but I have made progress, and I continue to make progress with every step I take. Instead of assuming that I have failed because I am learning a difficult lesson once more, I might embrace the experience as part of a long-term healing process that requires repetition and practice."

The following quote, from an anonymous source, sums up an approach that could be used to treat ourselves with more kindness and love: "View your life with KINDSIGHT. Stop beating yourself up about things from your past (decisions judged as bad). Instead of slapping your forehead and asking: 'What was I thinking,' breathe and ask yourself the kinder question, 'What was I learning?'"

> ". . . Oh Lord, heal me, for my bones are troubled. My [inner] self, [as well as my body] is also exceedingly disturbed *and* troubled . . . ."
> Psalm 6:2 (AMPC)

> "Hear me when I call, O God of my righteousness! You have relieved me in *my* distress." Psalm 4:1 (NKJV)

COMPLETION OF THE PAIN CAUSED BY LOSS

> "... A Man of sorrows and acquainted with grief ...."
> Isaiah 53:3 (NKJV)

I have just begun my fourth grief recovery workshop and I'm excited about it. It seems paradoxical that I could be "excited" about another grief workshop, but this one appears to be quite different from the others that I have attended this past year. Though the other workshops were helpful, they took me only so far; I believe this one will help me complete the pain of the loss caused by Kevin's death. I like the idea that it's about completion and not closure.

Many people talk about closure, but how can there ever be closure when your loved one was a huge part of the relationship—the other half? I don't ever want to "get over" Kevin, nor do I want to forget him. But I do want to move forward in my life and have loving, healthy relationships, instead of being stuck in the past. And I need some new tools to help me do that.

According to *The Grief Recovery Handbook* by John W. James and Russell Friedman, most professionals have addressed grief from a conceptual, intellectual perspective which has often left grievers with much understanding but very little recovery. Instead, the intent of this course is to focus on the emotional pain caused by death, divorce, and other losses. Grief is the conflicting feelings caused by the end of or change in a familiar pattern of behavior and is the normal and natural reaction to loss of any kind. In fact, there are more than forty other losses that one can encounter in a lifetime. I believe it's imperative to develop some helpful habits to deal with grief; according to the authors recovery is about discovering and completing the unfinished business in a relationship. It's been said that time heals all wounds, but it is what you do within time that will help complete the pain caused by loss.

I took some more of Kevin's things to Habitat for Humanity today and was very blue about it. Melancholy and heaviness, which I can't seem to shake, permeate my heart. Nine months ago Kevin passed away from cancer and in the first three weeks following his death I loaded up about 80 percent of his things and gave them away. I was still in shock and denial and I felt I needed to do it as quickly as possible, otherwise I might not be able to do it at all. And sure enough, I was right. It is much harder to do it now, nine months later, because my heart is very heavy with grief. I recognize that it is crucial for me to develop some new habits to deal with this grief. If I acquire the correct information, practice, and make the best possible choices, I believe that I will be able to recover from this significant loss. I am looking forward to discovering what some of those treasures might be, and I know I've been led to the right place to find them.

"... Weeping may endure for a night, but joy *comes* in the morning."
Psalm 30:5 (NKJV)

*We could never have guessed,
we were already blessed* . . . . —James Taylor

AFTERNOON COFFEE WITH VALERIE

> "No eye has seen, no ear has heard, no mind has imagined what God has prepared for those who love him." 1 Corinthians 2:9

I met my dear friend Valerie for coffee this afternoon at Panera Bread, and what a treasured time it was. After we had time to chat and catch up, I shared with her that I was writing essays about treasures I was daily receiving from God. She wanted to hear more, and so, without much prodding, I read her three of them. Valerie was stirred and very enthusiastic about those three essays. She requested that I send all of them to her. She also asked if she could email them to her coaching clients to encourage them in their daily walk with God.

Wow! That about blew me away when she said that the essays could benefit and inspire others, and that she could use them in her line of work. As we were talking, a well-dressed couple, strangers to us, came up to our table and said they had overheard us talking and liked what they heard. That gave me additional validation that maybe these essays could serve and be useful to others.

Valerie advocated for starting a blog and putting them "out there." A few weeks ago, another friend suggested that I sign up for a YouTube channel and read the essays online. Some other folks have recommended that I get them published. I wasn't interested in proceeding with any of their recommendations. I simply felt compelled to write.

Perhaps I'm ready to rethink my friends' counsel that I ought to make the essays available to others, especially if they could provide hope and reassurance of God's great love and care. My prayer will be that God brings others into my life who know how to do this technology and will set it up for me because I am no techie and am clueless about how to do any of the tasks my friends suggested. If it is God's will that my essays be public, then it will have to be up to Him to supply the ways and means, and I'm not going to worry or stress about it.

Some months ago when God first impressed upon me to start writing about His goodness and the many gifts He wants us all to experience, I agreed to put pen to paper and record the daily treasures that were rapidly materializing before my eyes. The more I became aware of them, the more there seemed to be. Opening my eyes and becoming more conscious of all these blessings were very helpful compared to walking around like a blind woman, oblivious to what was going on all around me.

I made a bargain with God (or at least I tried to) that He would take me out of this world to be with Him and my deceased loved ones as soon as I was finished with the essays. Since my husband had passed away six months before, and I was heavily grieving and mourning his loss, my longing and desire was to be with him as soon as possible. So, I quickly got busy writing about one treasure a day to complete the project as fast as I could.

Things often don't turn out the way we think they should. I've heard it said that God laughs at our little plans, especially when it comes down to telling God what to do. His plans are always so much bigger and more expansive than anything we can dream up. I think He has in mind for me to stay around a while longer because there is more work to be done on planet Earth, and more people to care about, love, and support.

"You are the light of the world . . . Let your light so shine before men, that they may see your good works and glorify your Father in heaven."
Matthew 5:14, 16 (NKJV)

IT'S SO MUCH MORE THAN MONEY

"... It is more blessed to give than to receive." Acts 20:35 (NIV)

When it comes to money management, Kevin was my greatest teacher. He saved at least ten percent, tithed ten percent, and gave liberally to those in need. Yesterday, I had an opportunity to follow in his footsteps and it gave me great pleasure to be able to do so.

In 2011, he loaned money to Sally, a friend of ours, so she could buy out her franchise and establish a business in her own name. Faithfully she paid $500 each month for six years and had only six months left on the principal. This week I received a call from her saying that she was selling her house, purchasing a different one, and needed to pay off her loan in order to proceed. I told her the amount of the payoff and she said she would put a check in the mail to cover it. I said that wouldn't be necessary because I wanted to forgive the remaining debt in Kevin's memory. I knew that's what he would have wanted, and I wished to honor him in this way. She was stunned and couldn't thank me enough for the gift. I have learned so much from Kevin about generosity and giving that it brings me great joy to pass on to others some of the legacy he left behind. My dear friend Kimberly has also taught me a great deal. She always brings a gift, wherever she goes. What a great role model! I have started to practice that kind of giving as well and was delighted to be the channel to Sally for the wealth that God provided.

Since I had the means to forgive the debt, The Prayer of Jabez came to mind. Verse 1 Chronicles 4:10 teaches us, "Jabez cried out to the God of Israel, 'Oh that you would bless me and enlarge my territory! Let your hand be with me . . . .' And God granted his request." Because God has also richly blessed me and enlarged my territory with innumerable treasures and pleasures, I appreciate being able to pass some of them on to others. Hebrews 13:16 (NKJV) says: "But do not forget to do good and to share, for with such sacrifices God is well pleased." It's not so much an admonition or a "have to do," but it truly does benefit the giver, and I have discovered that it is, indeed, more blessed to give than to receive.

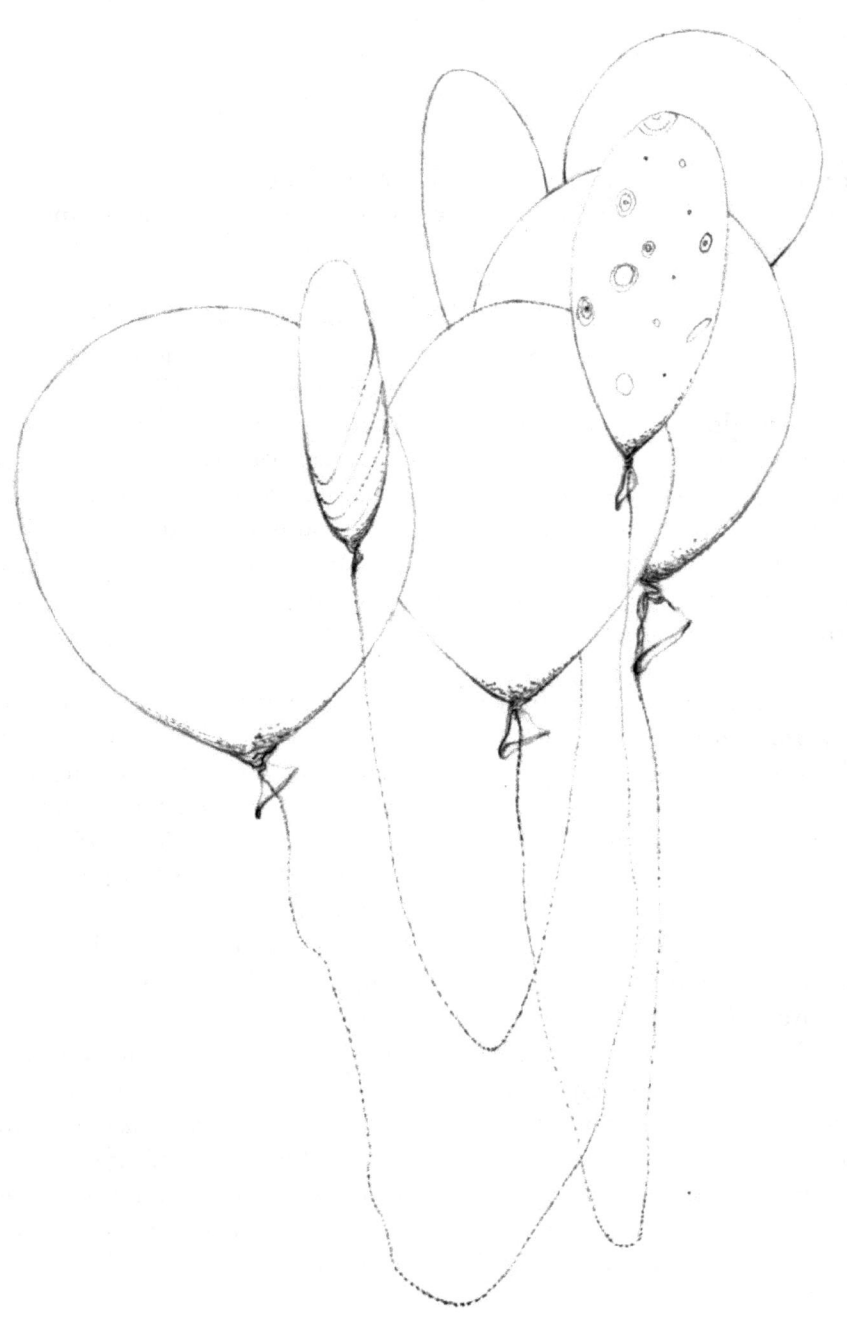

FEDEX

"I will command my blessing on you . . . ." Leviticus 25:21 (NKJV)

Yesterday, I stopped by a bank in Knoxville to get a release form signed and notarized. After the pleasant efficient woman finished stamping it with her seal, I asked if she knew where the nearest FedEx office was located. I was supposed to send the release back to a realty office in Chattanooga and was clueless as to where I might find a FedEx. As she began to give me directions, she exclaimed, "Well, here is a FedEx truck arriving this very minute and you can just give it to him."

I couldn't believe my good fortune, but here was yet another example of God supplying a request in my basket of needs. Slowly, I am becoming aware of God's presence in more areas of my life, even the seemingly mundane, trivial things. This encounter with the FedEx driver reinforced the assurance that God cares about me in every aspect of my life. "Look at the birds of the air, for they neither sow nor reap . . . yet your heavenly Father feeds them. Are you not of more value than they?" Matthew 6:26 (NKJV)

As I become more attuned to the ways that God is showing up in my life, I am daily rewarded with many instances of Him being smack dab in the midst of my journey, showering me with blessing upon blessing. The more I look for His footprints, the more I find. A stronger and deeper bond with Spirit ensues and increases my level of trust in Him. In Zephaniah 3:17 (NKJV), the Bible says, "The Lord your God in your midst . . . will rejoice over you with gladness, He will quiet you with His love, He will rejoice over you with singing." To imagine that he rejoices over me with gladness and singing dazzles my mind.

My response to this wonderful manifestation of His love can only be one of gratefulness and thanksgiving. He who knows the number of hairs on my head surely has only my highest best interests in mind. John 15:11 (AMPC), "I have told you these things, that My joy *and* delight may be in you, and that your joy *and* gladness may be of full measure *and* complete *and* overflowing." I will continue to immerse my mind and heart in these countless reassuring verses that proclaim the vast, boundless, inexhaustible love and care of God.

"If you, then, though you are evil, know how to give good gifts to your children, how much more will your Father in heaven give good things to those who ask Him!" Matthew 7:11 (NIV)

HOT WATER

"Oh, give thanks to the Lord! Call upon His name; Make known His deeds among the peoples!" Psalm 105:1 (NKJV)

I had been without hot water for two whole weeks. Something major had gone out in my hot water heater and since it was seventeen years old, there were no parts available to fix it. The 50-gallon tank I wished to replace it with had to be ordered online, and so a long wait ensued. My neighbors were kind enough to offer to let me use one of their showers, but I just didn't feel comfortable traipsing across the yard with all of my toiletries for two weeks. So, instead, I used my own shower and tried to get comfortable with cold water running down my body. For some reason it was the iciest on my back and I never could get used to it. It reminded me of when I had traveled in Europe in my early twenties, and it was common practice to shower outside in cold water with my bathing suit on. At any rate, I'm a lot older now and it felt much colder. Brrr!

Finally, the new tank arrived at Home Depot two days ago and the installer was able to put it in yesterday afternoon. This morning, for the first time in two weeks, I was able to shower in hot water and as it covered me from head to toe, it felt like a huge luxury. And what a luxury it is, to have hot water. It's a treasure, actually. It wasn't that many years ago in the USA that water had to be heated in a big pot on a wood-burning stove in order to take a warm bath, and everyone in the family took a bath in the same water, one right after the other. Pity the poor soul who was the last to bathe. How fortunate we are today to be able to take individual showers with hot water. It's something that I just took for granted because I'd been doing it for such a long time. But now, I vow to be grateful for this treasure from here on out.

There are some interesting facts about the invention of the hot water heater. In 306 AD, the Romans had large baths with heated hot water and though they weren't considered to be real water heaters, they were considered to be precursors to water heating; however, it took a number of years before actual water heaters, as we know them today, actually were invented. In 1868, English painter Benjamin Waddy Maughan patented the first residential water heater which used natural gases for heating the water. It didn't have a flue to vent the gas vapors and was therefore considered unsafe to use in homes. But 21 years later, in 1889,

Edmund Rudd took the next step forward in the invention of the modern water heater with the inclusion of safety features in Maughan's design. Then, it took a little over a hundred years for the golden era of water heater inventions to be ushered in: the 1990s. That was when electric water heaters, solar water heaters, and gas water heaters all came into existence and there is now a wide array from which to choose.

As I think of the treasures that are laid upon my doorstep every day, I am filled with gratitude and thanksgiving for a Father who dearly loves me and desires to bless me, as well as others. In every direction that my eyes gaze, I observe countless inventions that have been inspired by a Higher Power, inventions that lighten my load and make my daily life so much better.

"Glory and honor to God forever and ever . . . ."
1 Timothy 1:17 (TLB)

"Remember the wonders he has done . . . ."
Psalms 105:5 (NIV)

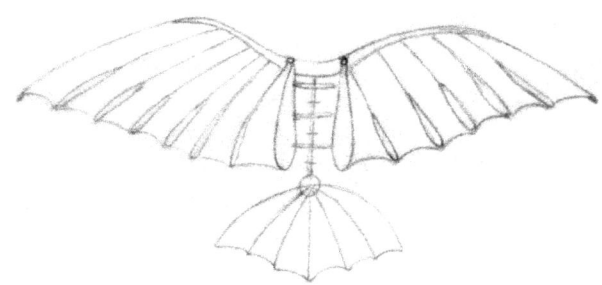

WRITING BUDS

"... Write them on the tablet of your heart." Proverbs 7:3 (NKJV)

I had lunch with treasured writing bud Teresa this morning, and we shared what we were each working on, as well as some of the resources we had been reading. It was a special time to encourage and inspire each other to keep on our respective journeys since writing can be a solitary, reclusive path. While she shared part of a novel she was writing about her relatives and where she fits into the story, I am writing essays about God's treasures. The genre doesn't matter, but the obstacles that get in the way of the writing process are similar for both of us.

For example, Teresa read the following from Ann Lamott's book, *Bird by Bird*, "We all ended up just the tiniest bit resentful when we found the one fly in the ointment: that at some point we had to actually sit down and write." Really?! That is a tough one, even though we both acknowledge that once we get started it isn't so bad, but it is the getting started part that is the problem. One must actually sit down at the keyboard and start typing, and then the words that are waiting to be released will at some point appear. It is much like sitting down at the piano to practice the scales, and then progressing to short easy pieces until one day it is time to tackle sonatas and concertos. That's also how it works with writing. Start with a prompt and write a paragraph then extend to a page, then pages, until finally a book that has been written.

Writing is also similar to training in sports. The way to get better and achieve success is to do it daily, just like athletes work out and prepare for their events. In her book *Writing Down Your Soul*, Janet Conner recommends a 4-Step Writing Process: 1) Set your **intention**, 2) Write with a **purpose**, 3) Follow this **process**, and 4) Make a **commitment** to use the wisdom received. And then it is all about practicing and putting in the time, which can't be stressed enough.

Both Teresa and I have found that one of the treasures of writing is the feeling of satisfaction that comes after the essay or book has been completed, much like giving birth and holding the newborn after it has been delivered. It is only after a piece has been written that we come to a better understanding of ourselves or some situation or event.

There is a kind of completeness/wholeness that is experienced in that which has been created out of mere words strung together to create sentences, then paragraphs, then pages, and finally books.

"In the beginning was the word . . . ." John 1:1

*Beauty is Truth, Truth Beauty,—that is all
Ye need to know on earth, and all ye need to know.*
—John Keats

ST. GEORGE ISLAND

"... There shall be showers of blessing." Ezekiel 34:26 (NKJV)

Exactly three months to the day that Kevin had passed away, I found myself driving down the interstate headed to Florida. Crying and sobbing all the way, I thought many times about turning around and heading back home to my comfort zone. But the kindness of my friend Nancy and her husband Tim kept me going. They invited me to go with them to a condo they had rented on St. George Island in Florida. I could not believe their thoughtfulness and generosity in asking me to go, a newly distraught widow who was sure to be a wet blanket on their vacation. As they led the way in their Jeep, I followed in my own car so that I could "escape" and go back home if I just couldn't handle it.

The following day I had more tears and felt extremely sorrowful with a deep longing for Kevin to be there with me. I prayed to God to give me strength and peace as I rode my bike and walked the beaches until dark. St. George Island is known as the "Forgotten Island" because only a few people seem to know about it or vacation there. It is a place of captivating beauty and enchantment. And this special place, placid and calm, with waves lapping gently to and fro along its shore, began to restore tranquility to my soul the more I walked and biked that first afternoon. Enjoying its beauty, I was slowly beginning to understand God's promise in Psalm 30:5 (NKJV): "... Weeping may endure for a night, but joy *comes* in the morning."

For the next three days my spirits lifted and I began to enjoy the area and its many blessings. During the day, I explored the island and its indestructible lighthouse with Tim and Nancy. This 72-foot high brick lighthouse had stood for 153 years on St. George Island until toppling into the Gulf of Mexico in 2005. I use the word *indestructible* to describe it because pieces of the lighthouse were retrieved, and in April 2008 the lighthouse's restoration was completed. It was an awesome structure to behold.

A couple of afternoons we explored Apalachicola, a small town near the island, with lots of little shops and great restaurants. From one of the shops, my companions surprised me with a beautiful necklace made with colored glass from the sea—a treasure, to be sure. In the evenings we cooked dinner, watched movies, and played games. It was truly a wonderful time that held a bit of respite from my grief.

I reached a turning point as a result of that trip because of the compassion and benevolence of my friends. I had first-hand experience, through this couple, with the Lord's goodness. As it says in Psalm 27:13 (AMPC), "[What, what would have become of me] had I not believed that I would see the Lord's goodness in the land of the living!" I saw it. I experienced it. And now I am more inclined than ever to believe in the reality of God's existence. He uses others to do His goodwill and I am so grateful and thankful. There were, indeed, countless showers of blessings.

THREE DAYS OF LA TREASURES

"Oh, how great is Your goodness . . . ." Psalm 31:19 (AMPC)

I had a wonderful three-day trip to Los Angeles, California, thanks to a friend of mine. Viewing great art, paintings and exquisitely bronzed sculptures in architecturally beautiful buildings was the purpose of the adventure, and it was all that plus much more! My engaging, inquisitive companion also provided so many more awesome experiences: walking the Promenade of Santa Monica; eating luscious 1500 calorie cheesecake slabs; driving along the Pacific shore to watch the sun set; and seeing the house, streets, and schools where my friend grew up. All of these made for an amazing, magical time. But probably the best part was honestly sharing the thoughts and ideas swirling around in our minds, verbalizing the fragile emotional feelings of our hearts, and enjoying the tangible sensations of physical rapport which led to a very transcendent experience.

Of the four art museums, the first one we visited was the Los Angeles County Museum of Art (LACMA), the largest art museum in the western USA. It annually attracts about one million visitors and holds more than 150,000 works spanning the history of art from ancient times to the present. Built in 1965, it was the largest new museum erected after the National Gallery of Art in Washington, DC. Among its many treasures is a $500 million donation of art from businessman Jerry Perenchio in 2014. This 47-piece collection of works by Cezanne, Degas, Magritte, Manet, Monet, and Picasso is the largest gift in the museum's history and, according to the *Washington Post*, is "conceivably one of the greatest art gifts ever, to any museum." What a treasure it was to walk through the rooms and bask in the presence of these masters' gifts to the world.

The next gallery on our list was the J. Paul Getty Museum, which in 1982 became the richest in the world when it inherited $1.2 billion dollars. An hour-long guided tour took us into the Impressionistic Gallery where we viewed a number of paintings by Renoir, Monet, Manet, Gauguin, as well as Van Gogh's painting, *Irises*. There is also a nice collection of bronze sculptures located in one of the wings. The best part is that the museum is free to the public, but the Getty has not been without controversy. In the 1970s and 1980s the curator purchased antiquities of dubious provenance as well as a number of fake artifacts. The Getty has also been involved in controversies with Italy and Greece regarding proper title to some of the artwork in its collection related to trafficking in stolen antiquities.

From there we drove to Pasadena to view more art at the Norton Simon Gallery, as well as historical documents and artifacts at the Huntington Gallery Library. While in Pasadena we also visited Vroman's Bookstore, the oldest and largest independent bookstore for over 120 years in Southern California. The founder, Adam Clark Vroman, loved books and loved giving back to his community. During World War II, a number of books were donated and delivered to Japanese Americans interned at nearby camps. Even though some book distributors were fired upon by camp guards on several occasions, the bookstore continued to act on its philanthropy. Owners believed that putting the right book in someone's hands could change that person's life. What better place to bring treasured books filled with encouragement and hope than to an internment camp of innocent victims?

"Yet the Lord will command His loving-kindness in the daytime, and in the night His song shall be with me . . . ." Psalm 42:8 (AMPC)

ELEPHANT SEALS

"And God said, 'Let the waters swarm *and* abundantly produce living creatures, and let birds soar above the earth in the open expanse of the heavens." Genesis 1:20 (AMP)

Many treasures line a six-mile beach area north of the San Simeon Hearst Castle on the West Coast of California. Thousands of elephant seals congregate on these sandy beaches along CA Highway 1 in their rookery hangouts—a breeding colony for animals—for their mating rituals. The Piedras Blancas rookery (where 23,000 seals assemble) has become a world-famous attraction. These seals are never all in the rookery at the same time. In July and August hundreds appear, whereas January through May sees them arrive by the thousands. They migrate thousands of miles to this secluded beach twice a year. The best times to visit are in late January, late April, and late October. My travel companion Marsha and I had an awesome opportunity to see these magnificent creatures as they were giving birth.

It all started on November 25, 1990, when about two dozen northern elephant seals were spotted in a small cove near the Piedras Blancas lighthouse. Every year after that, the seals came back, increasing in population each time. With the birth of one pup in 1992, the numbers increased yearly until a peak of 5,300 was reached in the 2016 birthing season. Elephant seals had been heavily hunted in the eighteenth and nineteenth centuries for the oil from their blubber until they were nearly extinct with fewer than 50 left. Mankind's role as protector of the earth and its treasures was carelessly disregarded and ignored, and the elephant seals were nearly wiped out and destroyed. Their plight reminds me of Psalm 12:1 (AMP), which reads, "Save *and* help *and* rescue, Lord, for godly people cease to be . . . ."

Fortunately, God "loves righteousness and justice; the earth is full of the goodness of the Lord," according to Psalm 33:5 (NKJV). And in the twentieth century, both Mexico and the USA moved to protect elephant seals. By then the development of kerosene and refined petroleum also helped put an end to man's hunt for the animals, as they were no longer of any commercial value. Today, these massive earless ocean creatures, which get their name from the males because of their trunk-like nose, have grown to over 200,000 treasures (according to *E-Seal News*).

"Restore us, O God of hosts; Cause Your face to shine . . . ."
Psalm 80:7 (NKJV)

"Oh sing to the Lord a new song! For He has done marvelous things."
Psalm 98:1 (NKJV)

Once again, the verses in the Bible point to God's loving-kindness and mercy to restore and regenerate what we humans have a tendency to squander and destroy.

"God created great sea creatures and every living thing that moves, with which the waters abounded, according to their kind . . . And God saw that *it was* good. And God blessed them, saying, 'Be fruitful and multiply, and fill the waters and the seas.'" Genesis 1:21-22 (NKJV)

MONARCH BUTTERFLIES OF PISMO BEACH

" . . . it is your Father's good pleasure to give you the kingdom."
Luke 12:32 (NKJV)

When my dear friend Marsha and I were traveling on the Central California Coast, we happened upon a Monarch Butterfly Grove at Pismo State Beach. Thousands of beautiful monarch butterflies with orange, black, and white markings hang in clusters on the leaves and branches of eucalyptus trees of the myrtle family. Because the leaves hang downward, it is sometimes arduous to discern which ones are butterflies and which are leaves as the butterflies are so densely packed. Four telescopes focus directly on the clusters to provide visitors with a close-up view. The best time to see this spectacular natural phenomenon is from October to the end of February when 28,000 monarchs gather in their annual migration across North America. The treasure trove is open seven days a week, operates docent-led tours, and offers this natural beauty for all to enjoy. "Taste and see that the Lord is good.." Psalm 34:8 NIV)

We learned many interesting facts as we visited this spectacular habitat. For example, monarchs go through four developmental stages to complete their life cycle in 28 to 38 days.

Egg → Larva (Caterpillar) → Pupa (Chrysalis) → Adult (Butterfly)

This process (metamorphosis) begins after the female mates and lays her white, pinhead-size eggs under the surface of milkweed leaves, the plant species that is the host plant for monarchs. There are about 20,000 different species of butterflies, and since each species uses a different plant as its host, the earth's widespread abundance is impressively evident. "In Your presence *is* fullness of joy; At Your right hand *are* pleasures forevermore." Psalm 16:11 (NKJV)

It takes about four days for the monarch's eggs to hatch into larvae (caterpillars), which are so small they can barely be seen. During this stage, the caterpillar's only job is to eat (it gains about 2700 times its original weight) and shed (molt) its skin. It grows very fast, gobbling up enough milkweed leaves in one day to equal its body weight, and it sheds its skin a total of five times; a new, larger skin awaits it under the one that is shed. After the caterpillar is fully grown, it crawls to a safe place to construct a silk-like mat where it attaches itself. Then the caterpillar sheds its skin for the fifth time to pass to the pupa (chrysalis) stage where it will be miraculously transformed into a beautiful monarch butterfly. "God saw everything that He had made, and behold, it was very good." Genesis 1:31 (AMP)

The metamorphosis process for butterflies is similar to what I would call the "Four G" metamorphosis process for the transformation of human beings into creatures God intended us to be. The first stage, to "grasp" who we really are, is to take an inventory of our assets and defects of character: the good, the bad, and the ugly. Next, we ask for God's "grace" to transform our shortcomings and imperfections into virtuous qualities. Third is to offer "gratitude" and thanksgiving to God for doing for us what we could not do for ourselves. And finally, we allow the "goodness" of our true nature to emerge and shine forth into the world.

Grasp (our true condition) → Grace → Gratitude → Goodness

"[Not in your own strength] for it is God Who is all the while effectually at work in you [energizing and creating in you the power and desire], both to will and to work for His good pleasure and satisfaction and delight." Philippians 2:13 (AMPC)

PRESERVATION HALL NEW ORLEANS

"Trust in the Lord with all your heart and lean not on your own understanding." Proverbs 3:5 (NIV)

The best jazz that I have ever heard in my life was at Preservation Hall in the French Quarter of New Orleans. It was one of the many treasures that I experienced on my trip to Louisiana, and I am grateful that a good friend recommended this funky, bare bones place to me. The musical venue is a tiny little hole in the wall with no bar, no restroom, no microphones, and only two ceiling lamps. It was founded in 1961 to protect, preserve, and perpetuate Traditional New Orleans Jazz and the following endorsement from Louis Armstrong best sums up the place: "Preservation Hall. Now that's where you'll find all of the greats."

I nearly didn't get to enjoy the performance because I was too busy obsessing about a problem I had. When my good friend Nancy dropped me off at the Hall, I told her that after the concert I would check out some of the shops nearby and that she should call me after she had finished dinner with her daughter Sidney. My plan was to tell her where to find me. Well, lo and behold, it wasn't until after she'd driven off that I realized my cell phone wasn't in my purse and that I must have left it back at the apartment. I had no idea how she was going to be able to contact me, and since I didn't know her cell number, I became quite anxious and panic-stricken trying to figure out what to do.

Immediately I started to come up with all kinds of different plans. The first one was to ask the guy standing in line next to me to use his cell phone. The only phone number that I thought I might remember was for my friend Macy back in Tennessee. I thought if I got in touch with her, she could relay my problem to Nancy, whom she also knew. During the program I sat next to the man and his wife to wait for Macy's response, but unfortunately she did not call back or answer my text because she was not available.

The second scenario was to ask the office manager if he could pull up my email on his phone, and then I could contact Nancy directly by email. He told me to find him after the program and he'd see what he could do. (Later, I learned from Nancy that she rarely checks her email.) Next, I thought about taking a cab to Sidney's apartment where I was staying, but I couldn't remember her exact house number and wasn't sure if her roommate would be at home to let me in. And then, finally, I thought to pray and turn the situation over to God. I asked Him to please take care of this big, fat mess. I left it in God's hands and settled down to enjoy the show, which was fabulous!

After the concert I sought out the manager to try to download my email, but before I could find him I heard a voice from outside shouting, "Phyllis! Phyllis!" I thought it was for some other person standing near me who had my same name, but when I repeatedly kept hearing "Phyllis," I looked outside in the direction of traffic and there was Nancy, driving in her car with her daughter. They had called my cell, and when they didn't get an answer they decided to come directly to the theater to pick me up. God had indeed worked it all out, without any help from me, and my trust level in Him went up a notch. I was also very happy that He helped to put aside my fears so I could sit back and enjoy the show.

"Trust in the Lord . . . And He shall give you the desires of your heart." Psalm 37:3-4 (NKJV)

*There are only two ways to live your life.
One is as though nothing is a miracle.
The other is as though everything is a miracle.*
—Albert Einstein

HEALING FROM BROKENNESS

> "Behold, I was brought forth in iniquity; And in sin my mother conceived me." Psalm 51:5 (NKJV)

None of us comes into this world perfect; we are all born flawed and defective in some way. Even though it is futile, I still strive to be perfect and need constant reminders that perfection is not possible on this plane of existence. I need to let go of that unrealistic goal. Playwright and Novel laureate Eugene O'Neill aptly states, "Man is born broken. He lives by mending. The grace of God is glue." Basically, life is about healing from our brokenness, which can be done only through the grace of God. I cannot do it on my own power. But I am assured by Philippians 1:6 that God "who began the good work" within me will keep right on helping me grow in His grace.

As I think back over the past eight months since Kevin's death, I realize that my brokenness was even more pronounced after he had passed away, which left me feeling as if my heart had been ripped out of my body and had shattered into a thousand pieces that could never be put back together. And while it's true that it will never be the same as it was, I have been healing due to God's grace, the glue that is keeping me together.

God has used people with skin on to comfort, encourage, and console me. Over the past five months I have taken five trips with friends who have tremendously helped to alleviate some of the isolation, disconnection, and sorrow that I have experienced during this nightmarish ordeal. I am so grateful to those friends who accompanied me and roused my spirits, as well as to the many others who have helped smooth my path, for they have all bolstered, reassured and sustained me throughout this restoration process. Also, the three grief support groups I have attended during this time have been a safe place to share my feelings and pain and have helped to reestablish my balance and equilibrium.

Something slowly, but surely, is being reborn in me, and my hope is gradually being restored. The following quote from 13th century Persian poet and scholar Rumi gives me a sense of confident expectancy and sweet anticipation for what lies ahead: "Where there is ruin, there is hope for a treasure." And I have received an abundance of riches over these past eight months. As I focus on the many treasures my Higher Power daily places on my doorstep, I discern that God is always there for me and to support me in a state of gratitude, the key to recovery.

> "Consider it pure joy, my brothers and sisters, whenever you face trials of many kinds . . . ." James 1:2 (NIV)

> "Humble yourselves in the sight of the Lord, and He will lift you up." James 4:10 (NKJV)

AN AQUA BLUE TWO-WHEELER

"May you always be doing those good, kind things that show that you are a child of God…" Philippians 1:11 (TLB)

One morning, as I sat recalling all of the many treasures I had been receiving on a daily basis, my blue bicycle came to mind. Somehow I hadn't even thought of it as a treasure, perhaps because I'd been riding it for years I'd overlooked it, but this aqua-blue bike has given me so much pleasure over time.

I like to feel the wind blowing through my hair and rippling across my face as I jauntily roam around my neighborhood. A large golden-colored collie, lazing tranquilly in the sun, perks up his head when I call out to it, but otherwise continues his motionless repose as I pass by. Squirrels and chipmunks scoot out of my way as I head directly toward them. Small Pekes and poodles on leashes yip and yap and strain to escape from their owner's clutches to chase after my bike and me.

It is a glorious day in mid-February to enjoy nature's offerings. The limbs of leafless trees sway gently in the breeze and birds' nests can be clearly seen at this time of year. Puffy, white clouds slowly meander below the azure blue sky. Neatly maintained homes and exquisitely manicured landscapes add to the overall charming scene. My soul is encompassed and enhanced by all of this outward manifestation of beauty.

The icing on the cake is to be able to share the many treasures God brings into my life with friends, and they, in turn, often affirm God's graces with gifts of their own. This brings to mind my dear friend Caroline who presented me with a charming print of an aqua-blue bicycle with a tan, tightly woven basket full of lovely golden sunflowers and bright orange carrots. Now that combination of sunflowers and carrots may seem incongruous to you, but it's really not. We need both in our lives. We need food to provide nourishment and sustenance for our material bodies, and we need things of beauty to foster and encourage our spiritual selves. Caroline thoughtfully ordered this picture especially for me. She "heard" me when I spoke fondly of my bike and then actively responded with a concrete object of that treasure. She is always doing good, kind, and meaningful things for others. I cherish her friendship and the spiritual connection we share. I feel richly blessed and grateful for all of the treasures that God provides so generously and abundantly to us all.

"... we ask that you may be filled with the knowledge of His will in all wisdom and spiritual understanding; that you may walk worthy of the Lord, fully pleasing *Him*, being fruitful in every good work and increasing in the knowledge of God." Colossians 1:9-10 (NKJV)

THE BLUEBIRD OF HAPPINESS

"... you are of more value than many sparrows."
Matthew 10:31 NKJV)

About five months after Kevin passed away, when I was steeped in sorrow and grief, I received a beautiful bluebird pendant from my dear friend Macy. A small bird that fit loosely on a chain, it was a huge treasure that showed up exactly at the right moment it was most needed.

I was curious to know more about the bluebird and after a bit of research discovered that it was the perfect symbol for where I was on my heartbreaking journey. Bluebirds are thought by some to be symbols of the heavenly realm, and when one appears it might be bringing signs of departed loved ones. When we are feeling sad and bereft, the bluebird's spiritual essence comes to remind us that beauty is all around us and that we will be restored to peace and joy. To help mitigate our pain and suffering, bluebirds can remind us to count our blessings, write them down in a journal, and share them with others.

The history of the connection between the bluebird as the harbinger of happiness is a fascinating read. It is found in many cultures and may date back thousands of years. One of the oldest examples was found on oracle bone inscriptions of the Shang Dynasty between 1766 – 1122 BC. It wasn't until 1908 that it became a popular expression in our culture. The phrase "bluebird of happiness" was originally coined by playwright Maurice Maeterlinck in his 1908 play, *The Blue Bird*. In fact, it has become so popular that September 24 has been designated as "National Bluebird of Happiness Day" in the United States. Gifts are given on that day to wish happiness on the recipients.

A popular American song, "Bluebird of Happiness," written in 1934 by Sandor Harmati and Edward Heyan, was recorded twice by Jan Peerce and also by the Art Mooney Orchestra. In Russian fairy tales, the bluebird is a symbol of hope. Bluebird is a term that has become increasingly popular in corporate circles to signify new business opportunities, which seemingly come out of nowhere and fly through the window. And that's what my dear friend gave me: a beautiful bluebird. This precious symbol of hope and happiness helps get me through sleepless nights and interminable days and radiates a blessed reminder of the myriad treasures designed explicitly for me by my Higher Power. And I am so grateful!

> ". . . But not a single sparrow can fall to the ground without your Father knowing it. And the very hairs on your head are all numbered. So don't be afraid; you are more valuable to God than a whole flock of sparrows." Matthew 10:29 – 31 (NLT)

RAINBOWS

"Immediately I was in the Spirit; and behold, a throne set in heaven, and *One* sat on the throne... and *there was* a rainbow around the throne." Revelations 4:2-3 (NKJV)

Who isn't dazzled by a rainbow? I know I am, and I think it is one of the most colorful, mystical treasures on earth. The quote by poet and author Aberjhani, "Dare to love yourself as if you were a rainbow with gold at both ends," provides an excellent image of reflection that promotes greater self-esteem and love for oneself.

The rainbow's beautiful multicolored arc consists of seven major colors: red, orange, yellow, green, blue, indigo, and violet. It is actually a continuum of colors between red and violet with about 100 hues in between, and colors even beyond what the human eye can see. This meteorological phenomenon is caused by reflection, refraction, and dispersion of light in water droplets which can be seen from an angle related to a light source. If the light source is the sun, then the center of the circular arc of the rainbow will appear in the sky directly opposite the sun. The arc can be a full circle, but the observer sees only the part above the ground.

Rainbows are not a specific distance from the observer but are optical illusions that can never be reached. According to myth, the Irish leprechaun's secret hiding place for his pot of gold is at the end of the rainbow, which, of course, can never be attained, and hence will never be found. In his book *Weather Proverbs and Paradoxes*, William Jackson Humphreys explains some proverbs associated with rainbows have meteorological justifications. Examples are: "Rainbow at night, shepherd's delight; Rainbow in morning, shepherds take warning," "If there be a rainbow in the eve, It will rain and leave; But if there be a rainbow in the morrow, It will neither lend nor borrow," and "Rainbow to windward, foul fall the day; Rainbow to leeward, damp runs away." I heard some of those aphorisms growing up but never knew there was a logical basis for them if applied to northern temperate zones with a prevailing wind.

I love to walk outside or ride my bike when I sense a rain storm coming. There is something in the atmosphere that draws me outdoors to await the pitter-patter of raindrops falling from a dark, cloudy sky. I want to be present as soon as a rainbow appears amid the clouds, as it is one of the most spectacular light shows on earth. Rainbows are among the many treasures that our Higher Power uses to remind us of His great love and care for us and that we can always rely on and trust in His Word.

"I set My rainbow in the cloud, and it shall be for the sign of the covenant between Me and the earth." ". . . never again shall there be a flood to destroy the earth."
Genesis 9:13, 11 (NKJV)

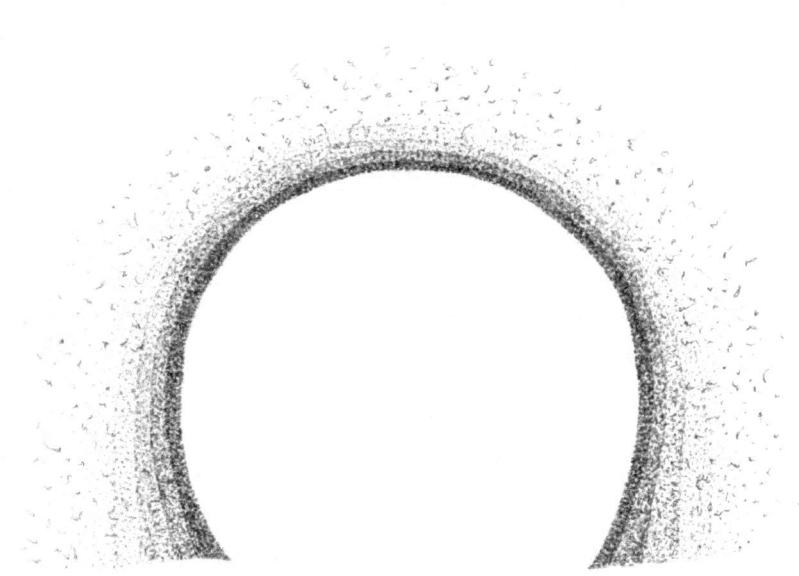

WOMEN'S EASTER BRUNCH

"A man *who has* friends must himself be friendly,
But there is a friend *who* sticks closer than a brother."
Proverbs 18:24 (NKJV)

On the Saturday before Easter, fifteen women came over for an Easter Brunch. Each woman brought a favorite dish to serve, as well as a beauty tip(s) for the face, hair, or body. As we went around the table eating scrumptious food and sharing our best tips, there was a consensus that drinking plenty of water, getting the right amount of sleep, eating healthily, consistently exercising, learning and exploring new things, and having a positive mindset were most important for aging beautifully with grace. In other words, cultivating wholesome, beneficial habits were keys to experiencing an enriched successful lifestyle which includes both inner and outer beauty.

After the meal and tips, we proceeded to the family room for the second part of the brunch. Those who wished to exhibit a creative endeavor they had worked on brought their project(s) along for a delightful "show and tell" time, an enjoyable experience for all. Kimberly showed us intricately woven, colorful wicker baskets constructed with rattan (also known as reed) and brooms that she had made. She also shared about the ice cream shop she had set up in the little town of Loudon, Tennessee, after she had learned how to make ice cream in Pennsylvania. Called "The Tick Tock Ice Cream Shop," it was so successful that it had been featured in *Southern Living Magazine* as a go-to destination for tourists. Teresa brought a beautifully framed painting of a winter scene that portrayed a snow-covered building surrounded by trees. She had this picturesque painting turned into 50 postcards to send out to friends and loved ones for Christmas using the online service *Shutterfly*. She also displayed a charming blanket she had quilted and read a captivating poem she had written.

Brenda read a speech she had prepared for a presentation she was to use to promote *Silent Scars*, a book she had authored. It tells her heart's journey about living with a Vietnam Veteran who suffers from PTSD (Post Traumatic Stress Disorder). This is a story about the toughest days of her life as she watched her husband struggle with the after-effects of an unpopular war that caused the deaths of many of his comrades.

Another friend, Lyle, brought an upholstered seat cushion she had recovered, as well as a slipcover she had just started to work on. Jeannie showed us a collage she had created and read a children's short story she had authored about a turtle and his shyness. Janet brought original jewelry she had designed and exhibited at craft fairs and other venues. I bought two of her necklaces, one for a friend's retirement and one for myself that had a brooch with a single pearl inserted inside a shell as the focal point, a stunning piece of work. Mary showed pictures of a butterfly quilt she had sewed and recounted about how it had come into being after her daughter's frightening hospitalization. And I sang a song entitled, "The Rose." It was a wonderful time of sharing, savoring, and treasuring the many talents of our gifted "sisters." The third event of the brunch revolved around Kimberly's five dozen eggs she had previously colored and brought for us to decorate, a very kind, loving thing for her to do. She is the type of friend who loves at all times (Proverbs 17:17). What a fun, fun time it was to paste on ears, eyes, noses, mouths, feet, and other body parts to make rabbits and all sorts of other little creatures. These awesome treasures were taken home as keepsakes (well, as long as you can keep an egg before it starts to smell) to grandchildren, husbands, and whoever might enjoy them.

It was a very special day to celebrate friendship and the many blessings I have received from these amazing, awesome women. I am so grateful and appreciative that God has brought us all together to love, honor, and care for each other. What an incredible, marvelous journey we are all on with pleasures and treasures galore to cherish, build beautiful memories, and hold dear.

> ". . . At Your right hand *are* pleasures forevermore."
> Psalm 16:11 (NKJV)

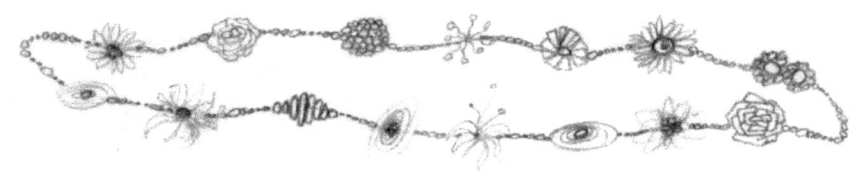

EASTER CELEBRATION

"... Love your neighbor as yourself ...." James 2:8 (NIV)
"Share with the Lord's people who are in need. Practice hospitality."
Romans 12:13 (NIV)

What a treasured time I had at Teresa and Dan's Easter celebration this year. As I was driving to their house, my phone began ringing and, seeing Teresa's name on my screen, I immediately thought, *Oh no, I must be late.* But no, she said she was just calling to check on me and see how I was doing. I felt very special to know I was being thought of, and it was a great beginning to the celebration that was about to occur with her and her family, as well as our other treasured friend Brenda, who was also coming.

When I arrived, I found Dan carving the rib roast and Teresa a little upset because the turkey wasn't done. She had put it in the oven the day before for a few hours and thought it could finish roasting on Easter, but it didn't quite work out that way as it just wasn't getting done. Even with turning the heat up and her sister tending to it, the turkey was not cooperating. They were calling it a bad turkey because it was causing angst and some not-so-pleasant feelings! Since I'm vegetarian, that didn't matter one little whit to me! I was much more interested in Teresa's sweet potato casserole, mandarin orange cake, and cupcakes. In addition, there was a broad array of food displayed on their massive island countertop. It literally was a feast, for the eyes as well as the stomach! Corn, peas, green beans, mashed potatoes, stuffing, gravy, and much more that couldn't possibly fit on my plate awaited, and I had a huge plate! I went back three times for her sweet potato casserole and added a couple of pounds to my frame, I'm sure. It was worth it, as it was the best I have ever tasted. The casserole (a Ruth's Chris Steak House recipe) was loaded with brown sugar, nuts, butter, and of course yams.

After the meal, we went outside to hide Easter eggs for the kids. Teresa must have had over a hundred eggs in her container; it was so much fun to find unique hiding places for them all, like water spouts, toy trucks, and tree gnarls, as well as bushes and tall grasses. The most fun was watching the kiddos run from place to place finding the eggs and gathering them into their baskets. They had such a great time that when it was over, three year old Gracie wanted us to hide them, again. So, once more we placed the eggs all over the yard and watched as the children delightfully gathered them a second time. I think that did the trick, because they didn't ask for a third time, though we would have been more than happy to accommodate them! Next, we followed the children to their play area where they were pushed on swings and helped down the tall slide. A little wading pool was set up for them to play in, but I think they had far more fun spraying each other with the water hose. Fortunately, they didn't aim for the adults. Caleb, Gracie's four-year-old brother, came running to us with an announcement that two-year-old Titan had taken off his diaper and was peeing in the pool. We turned around to look, and sure enough, he was peeing into the clear blue water which now had a touch of yellow in it! Caleb didn't want to go back in "that" pool, he said, so another urine-free pool was set up so that he could swim. But that didn't last too long, either. As soon as the pool was ready, Caleb and the others hopped back in, but this time the other kiddos were yelling that Caleb was peeing in the pool! Honestly, I never saw anything like it! Two very young lads marked their territory like a couple of dogs spraying fire hydrants, bushes, and trees! Males!!! Those cultural expectations and antics seem to start at such a very early age!!!

It was a beautiful, sunshiny day with a slight breeze blowing through my hair, just perfect for being outdoors, and I had such a lovely time. I am grateful for treasured friends like Teresa for asking me to spend the afternoon at her house. She knew that I would probably be missing Kevin, even more so at this time, and I was so appreciative for her invitation. When I got home, I was quite exhausted from all of the fun, but wouldn't have missed being a part of the celebration for anything. Many wonderful, precious memories will fondly be recalled for years to come of Teresa and Dan's hospitality, love, and generous spirit.

> "Behold, how good and how pleasant it is for brethren to dwell together in unity." Psalm 133 (APMC)

> "Be devoted to one another in [brotherly] love . . . ."
> Romans 12:10 (NIV)

THREE TREASURED GARDENS

"Then God said, "Let the earth bring forth grass, the herb *that* yields seed, *and* the fruit tree *that* yields fruit according to its kind, whose seed *is* in itself, on the earth"; and it was so. . . . And God saw that *it was* good. [13] So the evening and the morning were the third day."
Genesis 1:11-13 (NKJV)

The best time of the year to visit Knoxville is in April as this is the month that the Dogwood Arts Festival takes place in all its glory. Incomparable beauty can be seen while driving on the "marked in pink" dogwood trails during the month and/or walking three magnificent gardens featured for one weekend only, every year.

The day I chose to tour the gardens started out with rain; however, by 1:00 p.m. the rain had stopped, the sun had come out, and it was time to start my adventure. The first garden I chose to explore was GATOP (God's Answer To Our Prayers) which had been aptly named by Lloyd and Virginia Pease who had prayed they'd find a home that overlooked both water and mountains. In1941, they found what they had been looking for and moved from Chattanooga to Knoxville onto this property that had beautiful views of the Tennessee River and the Great Smoky Mountains.

In 1971, Dr. Alan Solomon purchased the property and over the last 45 years has devoted his time and efforts, along with other skilled gardeners and craftsmen, to enhance and preserve the natural beauty of this heavily wooded acreage located two miles from the heart of Knoxville. He has planted extensive collections of native and rare plant specimens and also, as a result of membership in the American Conifer Society, about 350 varieties of conifers. Over 800 tons of limestone have been used to build walls, steps, and ponds; it's no wonder that this property has been included in the Smithsonian Institution's Archives of American Gardens. Additional features of the property include small, medium-size, and large sculpted frogs that overlook the ponds, as well as numerous stainless steel, bronze, and stone sculptures that Dr. Solomon has purchased over the years. This lush, impressive landscape was also featured in the 2015 Dogwood Arts Festival and it's quite understandable why it would be featured again.

The second garden I investigated was the Savage House and Garden located in the Fountain City community of Knoxville. Exactly one hundred years ago Arthur Savage began his garden, impressed after a visit to his native England. He began by building stone walls, ponds, arbors, and a pagoda which reflected a Japanese influence. Savage, known as "the father of rock gardening in Knoxville," also erected two "Irish" water towers amid thousands of trees, shrubs, and perennials. The springtime features hydrangeas, wildflowers, and bulbs. In 1937, the Savage Garden was damaged by a tornado, and it wasn't until 1986 that it was sold to Bill Dohm and Patty Cooper, who have since renovated the garden and restored its fountain. The house was designed in the bungalow/craftsman style, and both the house and its garden are listed on the National Register of Historic Places.

The third and final garden to be seen was the Baxter Garden, also located in the Fountain City community of Knoxville, about two miles from the Savage Garden. Initial plantings were installed 25 years ago and now more than twenty acres of gardens have been designed, landscaped, and planted atop Black Oak Ridge. Multiple gardens with various themes comprise the acreage. One of the features is a beautiful fountain supported by a rendition of The Three Graces, which represent joy, charm, and beauty. The installation was sculpted by Antonio Canova. It is located between the White Garden (plants in this garden bloom white throughout the year) and the Bluebird Garden (cotoneaster shrubs and viburnums attract bluebirds as they produce the bluebirds' favorite berries in great abundance).

Statues of famous people are located in another garden. They include Mark Twain, Aristotle, Abraham Lincoln, and Thomas Jefferson, to name just a few. And then there is a maze composed of 780 columnar yew shrubs. It took me forever to reach the center where a small fountain and a seating area await those fortunate enough to find it. I got lost trying to find my way out, but fortunately the rain held off until I reached the exit and got back to the car.

Three spectacular gardens, verdant treasures all viewed one splendid Saturday afternoon, are generously opened to the public by their owners. Kudos to Knoxville's good-hearted locals and the enchanting gardens they share.

"But do not forget to do good and to share, for with such sacrifices God is pleased." Hebrews 13:16 (NIV)

MANNA

"... in the morning the dew lay all around the camp. And when the layer of dew lifted, there, on the surface of the wilderness, was a small round substance, *as* fine as frost on the ground."
Exodus 16:13-14 (NKJV)

There must be something important about the early morning hours. It was when God provided manna as sustenance for the children of Israel to eat. It is also when the ocean deposits its shells upon the shore for beach combers to gather. And it is when the birds start their joyful tweeting and singing to awaken the world to a brand new day.

I have found that the morning hours are also a good time to meditate and commune with God. When I seek my Higher Power first thing in the morning, my day goes a lot better. David declared in Psalm 63:1 (NKJV), "O God, You *are* my God; early will I seek You . . . ." It is a treasure to receive spiritual wisdom and insights before I get started in the activities of the day. And even though I know the value of doing this early, I often don't do it until the afternoon or evening hours. That's not a bad thing, but if I sought those blessings earlier, then I could pass them on to others I meet during the day who could also use them.

When I walk, I often do one of the following: pray, meditate, or read spiritual books. Exercise and spiritual connection through multi-tasking seem to work very well for me. Mantras also keep me attuned to the Divine. Two that I currently use are "I trust You, God, in all circumstances and situations. Thank you," and "I treat myself and others with loving-kindness and compassion, which comes only from You, God. Thank you."

Trust and thankfulness go hand in hand. They are a circular duo. The more I practice trusting God, the more grateful I am that I can find Him trustworthy in all circumstances. The more thankful I am, the more trust that seems to engender. The following scripture verse is a good reminder for me to keep up the practice of trust. "Trust in the Lord with all your heart, And lean not on your own understanding; In all your ways acknowledge Him, And He shall direct your paths." Proverbs 3:5-6 (NKJV) And these two verses remind me to continue the practice of thankfulness. "Rejoice always," and "in everything give thanks; for this is the will of God . . . ." 1 Thessalonians 5:16, 18 (NKJV)

When I remember to focus on these two key concepts the first thing in the morning, as well as throughout the rest of the day and evening, these beliefs slowly get embedded into my brain and create new neuro-pathways. The practice of trust and thankfulness covers over the ruts of fear and ingratitude that have been etched in my brain throughout the years, and like gravel that fills in the ruts in a road, the journey becomes smoother and more pleasant.

". . . joy comes in the morning." Psalm 30:5 (NKJV)

TOTAL SOLAR ECLIPSE

"And God said, 'Let there be light.'"
"God called the light 'day,' and the darkness he called 'night.'"
Genesis 1:3, 5 (NIV)

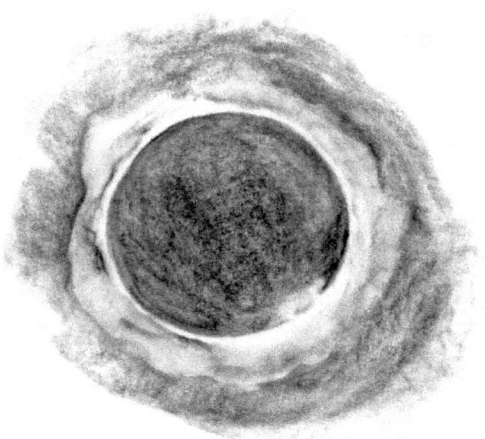

On August 21, 2017, the most glorious event I've ever seen in my lifetime occurred in the skies of Lenoir City: a total solar eclipse. What an awesome sight it was to behold! It traversed a narrow band of sky from the Pacific to the Atlantic, which began in Oregon and ended in South Carolina, before it crossed over the Atlantic and ended near Africa at sunset. In the United States, it lasted just 94 minutes and was the nation's first coast-to-coast total solar eclipse since 1919, nearly a century. The last total solar eclipse which occurred in the continental USA, but was not a coast-to-coast event, happened 38 years ago in 1979, before almost half of the Americans alive for this 2017 momentous event were even born.

Millions of people from across the nation and other countries poured in ahead of time to gain a place for themselves within the path of totality to watch this amazing, spectacular show as the moon's shadow raced across the land at 2,000 mph. So, what exactly is a solar eclipse? It happens when the moon casts a shadow on Earth, fully or partially blocking the sun's light in some areas. If the sun and moon don't quite line up, it is a partial eclipse. If they completely align, it is called a total eclipse. The sun is actually about 400 times larger in diameter than the moon, but since the moon is about 400 times closer to Earth than the sun, they appear to be about the same size in the sky. The moon has an apparent size that just barely covers the sun completely, but it's just an illusion.

Every eclipse begins at sunrise at some point in its track and ends at sunset about halfway around the world from the starting point. Eclipses cannot be seen from either the North or South Poles. Totality can last a maximum of seven minutes and 30 seconds, and during this time local animals and birds often prepare for sleep or behave confusedly. To view this phenomenon, it is essential that the eyes be protected with special eclipse-viewing glasses, as permanent eye damage can result without them. These glasses must be kept on until the moon completely covers the sun. Then, they can be removed during the totality phase, but must be put back on before the sun returns. If viewing outside the path of totality, it is never safe to take the glasses off.

I threw a party at my house for about 25 guests and everyone was astonished by what they observed. From beginning to end, the eclipse lasted nearly three hours. We watched as the moon first nicked the sun and as the bite grew steadily larger until the sun became a narrow crescent; daylight still appeared bright. Then, about ten to fifteen minutes before totality, there began to be an eerie quality of daylight, which diminished minute by minute. The shadows grew sharper and the temperature started to quickly drop. Just before totality, the sunlight looked strangely different, not day and not night, and the sky displayed a gradient of colors. At totality, which lasted about two minutes, it suddenly became dark, and the outdoor solar lights immediately came on. A 360-degree sunset could be seen. The birds acted strangely. Thinking it was nighttime, they stopped their chirping and looked for places to roost. Other unusual things can be seen during an eclipse, like shadow bands, Bailey's beads, and diamond ring flashes. It was a marvelous supernatural treasure incomparable to anything I've ever witnessed.

"The heavens declare the glory of God . . . ." Psalm 19:1 (NKJV)

God's greatest gifts puts man's gifts to shame.
—Elizabeth Barrett Browning

MY BROTHER PASSED AWAY

"The last enemy to be destroyed is death." 1 Corinthians 15:26

"Are you going come with me when I die?" "Are you going come with me when I die?" My brother repeated that question over and over to me when I would call him on the phone until finally I said, "No, I will not come with you when you die." And then it dawned on me what he was trying to say. He meant: "Are you going to come to my funeral when I die?" I told Bob that I wanted to come see him before he died and that I already had purchased my ticket to come out to Bismarck to visit him on August 9. No, I did not want to come to his funeral; I wanted to come talk to him in person and see him while he was alive. Bob had a form of dementia that made it difficult for him to find the words he was trying to convey, but I could tell that he was grateful when I finally understood his request.

As it turned out, I received a phone call from Bob's wife, Charlene, on July 20 telling me that I needed to come out immediately. She had just spoken to Bob's oncologist and the doctor said that Bob didn't have much time left. The plan had been to give Bob a stronger chemo, but he was deteriorating so rapidly that nothing could stop the downward progression of his illness. My brother had undergone open heart surgery in February, but his esophageal cancer was not detected until the end of May, and by then it was in its fourth stage. It was terminal, and nothing could be done except to prolong the pain, or so it seemed to me. He had already had chemo and radiation treatments in June, which did not help, and so the doctor planned to use a stronger chemo. Fortunately, my brother passed away before he had to endure any more torturous treatments. He was unable to swallow, which created excruciating pain for him, as well as his loved ones who witnessed his constant struggle just to swallow his saliva.

I took the first available flight out of Knoxville on July 21. Charlene and Bob's six children gathered around Bob's bedside, said their goodbyes, and gave him permission to go. But when they told him that I was coming, they said that he perked up even though he was unconscious when he heard that I was on my way. Sadly, my plane was one and a half hours late in the final home stretch, and during that time interval my brother passed away. It is ironic that my plane was early on all of my other connections, but the final connection from Minneapolis to Bismarck made me too late to see my brother before his spirit left his body. I was sorely disappointed; however, I believe that it was all in God's plan and happened as it was meant to happen. My brother wanted me there for his funeral and his wish was granted. Had I gone to see him sooner, I might not have gone back for the funeral.

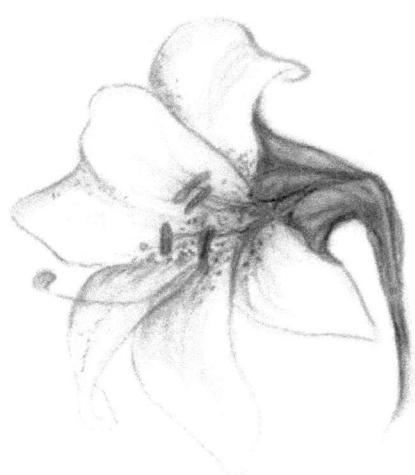

Bob had a strong faith in God; his minister went up daily to see him in the hospital and read God's marvelous promises as my brother slowly diminished in strength and vitality. The following verse can be one of great comfort to those facing death: "In My Father's house are many mansions; if *it were* not *so*, I would have told you. I go to prepare a place for you. And if I go and prepare a place for you, I will come again and receive you to Myself; that where I am, *there* you may be also." John 14:2-3 (NKJV)

There is a treasure in this situation that I would like to note. God prepared my heart in love, ahead of time, for reconciliation with my brother. For years, Bob and I had been estranged and hadn't communicated with one another. A couple of months before he was diagnosed with cancer I felt a strong tug on my heart to talk with him and try to straighten things out between us. Once I heard that he had cancer, I knew the time was right to call him. I talked to him and sent cards every day that he was consciously aware; fortunately, we made our amends during this time.

What a huge gift it was for both of us from God. I will always remember Bob as my "sweet little bro" whom I taught to read and write before he went into first grade. He was a smart and precocious child, and I taught him everything I learned in first and second grade before he got there. The teachers didn't quite know what to do with him because he was ahead of everyone in the first two grades.

Our parents didn't want him to skip a grade, and since he didn't need to do any homework, he had lots of time for extracurricular activities, like making model airplanes and cars. Bob's intellectual capacity was outstanding, and he graduated valedictorian of his class.

Unfortunately, after high school Bob had many relational difficulties, which could be attributed to the limitations of having grown up in a dysfunctional family environment. Even though life, at times, was so painful for Bob and others, it was perhaps due to a deficiency in and lack of healthy emotional skills that were not taught to him in childhood. Given those inadequacies, I believe you did the best you could, Bob. May you rest in peace.

"He will swallow up death forever, And the Lord God will wipe away tears from all faces . . . ." Isaiah 25:8 (NKJV)

CANCER CHEMO BAGS

"'Comfort, yes, comfort My people!' Says your God."
Isaiah 40:1 (NKJV)

I had coffee with my friend Kelly this morning. Kelly is an eight-year breast cancer survivor and is filled with gratitude that she is doing well. As a way of giving back, she makes chemo bags for cancer patients and distributes them to patients at their first chemo treatments. She fills tote bags with various things that oncology patients will need as they go through their procedures and regimen. Having been through it herself, she knows exactly what the bag should contain. Since cancer patients are prone to infections, she includes handy-wipes as well as hand sanitizer bottles. For dry lips, she puts in ChapStick or Vaseline. To refocus the patients' thoughts and to take their minds off the treatment, she includes crossword and Sudoku puzzles. A pen and notepad for taking notes when their brains are fuzzy, as well as many other treats are also included in each tote.

A sizable source of discomfort for many in treatment is the feeling of being cold much of the time, freezing, actually, so Kelly makes fleece blankets for patients. The blankets envelop and wrap their bodies to keep them warm. I remember a time when I had to take my husband Kevin to Emory Hospital in Atlanta, Georgia, to see an oncologist. The night before his appointment, we stayed in a motel close to the hospital, and Kevin just couldn't seem to get warm. So, even though it was July and sweltering outside, I turned off the air conditioning, turned up the heat to 90 degrees, and requested four blankets from the front desk. After he warmed up, his teeth stopped chattering, his body stopped shivering, and he was finally able to peaceably go to sleep.

Since my husband's death from cancer, I have felt an inner desire to do something to try and help folks with cancer endure their agonizing ordeal, and so I asked Kelly if I could join up with her and make personalized encouragement cards to go into the tote bags. She very graciously accepted my offer and I was thrilled. I also asked if there was anything I could do to help out with the resources she regularly purchased, and she said that I could buy some fleece, since it was expensive and the most costly item in the bag. I was very happy that I could be useful and supportive in this way. We immediately left the coffee shop for a cloth shop where Kelly helped me pick out some material. She suggested a patterned fleece for one side and a solid color on the other side, so that it would look cheery for the patient, and she also offered to teach me how to make the blankets so I could help warm the patients' bodies.

I came home all excited and immediately started making encouragement cards. It was excellent timing, too, because shortly after I designed the first one, I received a text from my dear friend Mary that a friend of hers had just been diagnosed with stage IV breast cancer. She requested cards and scarves to help cheer her friend up. So, the first card will be sent out in the morning, to Mary's friend Amanda.

Serving the needs of others is one of the best methods for taking me out of my own pain and misery. I am so grateful that God is using me in this way, and it is a treasure beyond comparison. I believe this is God's will for my life, presently, and it brings me a great deal of peace and joy to be able to serve.

> "But do not forget to do good and to share, for with such sacrifices God is well pleased." Hebrews 13:16 (NKJV)

HEALING A BROKEN HEART

"He heals the brokenhearted and binds up their wounds."
Psalm 147:3 (NIV)

Things were not working out in a fairly new relationship that I was in and I was devastated, but I knew it was time to let it go l. It was my third loss for the year. First, my husband, Kevin, who died from cancer a year ago; second, my brother, Bob, who passed away from cancer a few weeks ago; and third was this loss of a relationship. I was leveled to the ground and wiped out, totally emotionally overwhelmed with feelings of tremendous sadness and bereavement.

Fortunately, God provided me with three opportunities to serve others, which helped to alleviate some of my angst. In the first, my friend Mary was at the hospital for her boyfriend's operation and requested something to eat and drink. I brought up some food and drink from Panera Bread, and I spent the afternoon with her to help pass the time while waiting for her boyfriend to come out of recovery and be assigned a hospital room. She was very appreciative and grateful that I could be there with her, but I was even more so, in that it took my mind off my own pain and suffering, if even for just a little while.

The second service opportunity came when I had coffee with my friend Brooke the next day. She was going through a rough spot, as we all do, and I was able to listen as she poured out her heart. I have heard it said that the greatest gift we can give another is to listen from our hearts. But this experience was a gift that I actually received as well because it took my mind off myself for a bit as I focused on my friend's angst and distress. Brooke has been there for me on numerous occasions with texts, cards, and calls to encourage and support my lonely journey, which helped a lot, as I continued to sorely miss Kevin.

The third situation involved meeting with a friend who was in anguish about her upcoming move. She had tried to get a job in Knoxville for a long period of time, and nothing had ever worked out. She knew that it was God's plan for her to move out of state and back to her parents' house, but she didn't want to go and leave all of her friends behind. This third time that I sat with a friend and listened to her ordeal filled me with gratitude as I realized that service to others was a key to alleviating some of my own pain and misery.

What a treasure it was to realize that when I help bear the burdens of others, I start to get better.

"Bear one another's burdens . . . ." Galatians 6:2 9 (NKJV)

". . . You shall weep no more . . . ." Isaiah 30:19 (NKJV)

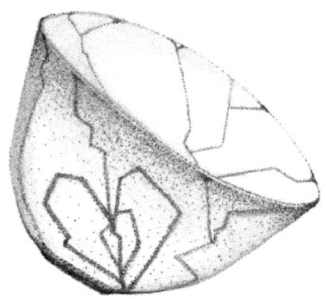

KEENING

"For in the day of trouble He will hide me in His shelter; In the secret place of His tent He will hide me; He will lift me up on a rock." "Teach me Your way, O Lord, And lead me on a level path . . . ."
Psalm 27:5, 11 (AMP)

I woke up this morning in terrible emotional pain. I knew I needed to do something to distract myself from the pain I was feeling because it was just getting worse. So, I made a Wal-Mart run and picked up some groceries for the weekend. When I got home, the tears started coming down in buckets. I was heartbroken and forlorn, thinking about the three huge losses I had recently suffered – my husband's death, my brother's death, and the loss of a relationship that I wanted so badly to work. I couldn't stop crying and the tears turned into gut-wrenching sobs.

It was then that I remembered a magazine article my friend Lyle had given me entitled "How to Lament." Written by Malia Wollan, the piece was is in the August 6, 2017 issue of *The New York Times Magazine*. This article was actually a guide on how to effectively lament one's losses, and I knew that I needed a very potent method to express my grief. James M. Wilce, a professor at Northern Arizona University who studies lamentation, or what he calls "melodic wailing," is quoted in Wollan's article. He states, "You must have visible tears. Wet cheeks are the minimum. In some places, funeral keeners throw themselves to the ground, sway their bodies or beat at their chests. It has to feel raw. Go on for five minutes or five hours – it's up to you. These age-old, song-like wailing traditions that have gone on for centuries are found worldwide, but they're disappearing from many places." I threw myself into this type of keening and wailing and discovered that it was a very healing, cathartic way to mourn and express my grief.

As I was nearing the end of this process, my friend Kelly called and asked me for a friend's phone number. I asked her, between sobs, if she had a few minutes to talk. She immediately suggested we meet at Panera Bread. Kelly was God with skin on, a wonderful treasure, and she listened patiently as I shared my grief. She also brought with her a blanket for a chemo patient that needed to be tied around the edges and asked if I would do it.

I was grateful for her request because doing something for someone else is one of the quickest ways to get out of one's own agony and sorrow.

"My God, my God, why have You forsaken me? Why are You so far from helping me, and from the words of my groaning?"
Psalm 22:1 (AMP)

"Show me your ways, Lord, teach me Your paths."
Psalm 25:4 (NIV)

"All the paths of the Lord are mercy and steadfast love . . . ."
Psalm 25:10 (AMPC)

ENERGY, PEP, AND ENDORPHINS – VITAL TREASURES

"He brought me up out of a horrible pit . . . , out of the miry clay, And set my feet upon a rock, steadying my footsteps *and* establishing my path. He has put a new song in my mouth, a song of praise to our God." Psalm 40:2-3 (AMP)

It started off as a depressing kind of day. I ruminated about all the losses that had piled up for me in the past year, and I felt lost and forlorn. Even the crossword puzzles didn't help, and I didn't want to make greeting cards to help someone else when I was the one in need. I anticipated nothing but loneliness and despair ahead of me and on into the future, and I polished that train of thought to perfection as I rehearsed it over and over in my mind.

I knew that if I walked and did my daily meditation readings that my mindset would improve, but I just couldn't get motivated to take care of myself. Joshua 1:9 (NKJV) was waiting for me, but I was unaware of it until much later in the day, when I finally did turn to God for help. " . . . do not be afraid, nor be dismayed, for the Lord your God *is* with you wherever you go." I certainly needed that reminder first thing in the morning as I forced myself to get out of bed, but alas, I didn't seek my Higher Power to alleviate my suffering until after I had made myself thoroughly miserable.

Finally, I got myself up off the couch and went downstairs to sweep off the patio and wash the windows. Some friends were coming over in a few days to see the Total Eclipse which would last for two whole minutes and wouldn't show up again in my life-time. Since I was having guests, I needed to make things presentable both inside and out, as I wanted friends to be comfortable and enjoy the experience. After a couple of hours of work, I began to feel better. As I exercised my muscles, my endorphin level started to rise, and in turn began to break me out of my depression.

At that point, I was able to ponder some of the treasures my High Power had bestowed upon me. First of all, I was grateful for the energy, pep, and vitality that were available to me to be able to do the housework. Second, I was appreciative that God equipped me with endorphins to help alter my moods when I get discouraged and disheartened. Third, I was thankful for my Higher Power doing for me what I could not do for myself and that I was pulled out of my depression and restored to sanity, where I could return my focus to the blessings all around me.

At last, I recognized my need to do my spiritual readings which would help reinforce the gifts I had just perceived. The first one I encountered was Proverbs 17:22 (AMPC): "A happy heart is good medicine *and* a cheerful mind works healing, but a broken spirit dries up the bones." How relieved I was to have my spirit renewed and reestablished. When God infuses me with His strength, I feel that I can be ready for anything that He asks of me. To know what that is, I pray for the knowledge of His will for my life and the power to carry it out.

> "I have strength for all things in Christ Who empowers me."
> Philippians 4:13 (AMPC)

GOLD MEDALLION DAY

> "... he is a new creation; old things have passed away; behold, all things have become new. Now all things *are* of God...."
> 2 Corinthians 5:17-18 (NKJV)

A friend received her gold medallion in Alcoholics Anonymous (AA) this afternoon from her father. His eloquent speech lauded and commended his daughter's extraordinary feat to become and stay sober over this past year, and he was thrilled to present her with a one year chip to recognize her sobriety for not taking a drink or a drug in the last twelve months. My friend quickly followed up his speech with one of her own, thanking both her dad, her mother, her close friend, and her AA friends for staunchly supporting and encouraging her on this arduous recovery journey.

I was thrilled to be there with another dear friend to behold this outstanding accomplishment, the transformation that had taken place from that of a dingy, drab chrysalis into a beautiful, colorful butterfly of a young woman. She glows with radiance and inner joy and is a testament to the AA program that changes lives with the help of a Higher Power.

Only God has the power to change lives and only He can make all things new, again. It first happened with the friend's dad 27 years ago. He got sober soon after his little girl was born; it was then that he realized he could lose her, as well as his entire family, if he continued to drink. He recognized that he was an alcoholic and that he couldn't stop drinking on his own. He needed help, so he turned to AA. When alcoholics admit their utter defeat and powerlessness over alcohol, they can begin their journey into sobriety. That is the first step into a new life if they so choose, and that is what he chose to do, which benefited not only him, but also his whole family.

It was very touching when my friend shared that she, too, wanted to be sober for her two children. She said that she was able to drive her five-year-old son to kindergarten and get him started in his new school year as a sober mom, and she was delighted and so happy to be granted this gift. She was also ecstatic that she had chosen this path of abstinence, for now she was able to be there for her children and connect with them on a level that would not be possible if she were still drinking and/or using.

Her mom has not only been a great influence on her daughter, but also on the entire family. She tirelessly prays for their welfare and well-being, and she diligently works an admirable 12-Step Al-Anon program, herself. She doesn't just talk the talk. She walks the walk as she daily practices the principles of the program in all her affairs. Both of the young woman's parents are great role-models for emotional as well as physical sobriety as they carry the message to others with this disease. I feel very blessed and grateful to be a part of this loving and caring family. They are a great and valued treasure, for sure!

"Admit your faults to one another and pray for each other so that you may be healed. The earnest prayer of a righteous man has great power and wonderful results." James 5:16 (TLB)

"He restores my soul." Psalms 23:3 (NKJV)

Through the crack created by my sorrow and loss, I can opt to let all the blessings (treasures) that God intends for me, to come into my life.
—Phyllis March

BREAST CANCER

> ". . . He gives to all life, breath, and all things. . . in Him we live and move and have our being. . . ." Acts 17:25, 28 (NKJV)

A year and a half after Kevin died, I felt this inner nudge to get a mammogram. It had been over two years since my last one and because I had been caught up in Kevin's care, I had chosen to forego my yearly exam. I called my doctor's office to set up an appointment. I sailed through the mammogram, but the ultrasound that accompanied it showed I had a small mass. Because it was so tiny, it was difficult to stage and determine the type of cancer. I waited what seemed like an eternity for the pathology report, and finally the doctor called with the diagnosis. I had non-invasive ductile cancer in one of my breast ducts. It did not seem that consequential to me, and my reaction was that of exuberance. My friends all thought I was crazy since I wasn't wringing my hands and pounding my chest because I had just been diagnosed with the C-word, *Cancer*.

You see, I had wanted God to take me after my husband died. I had been grief-stricken and lonely, and it took monumental effort to put one foot in front of the other. Now, I felt that God was giving me a choice. If I declined the surgery that was recommended, the cancer would grow, I would die, and it wouldn't be long before I'd see God, Kevin, and all of my loved ones. But, what if God had more work for me to do here and would like me to stay and carry that out? In my heart of hearts I knew that was what God wanted of me, and since I truly wanted to be in God's will for my life, I chose to listen to that still small voice telling me to continue to love and serve others here on earth. ". . . through love serve one another . . . 'You shall love your neighbor as yourself.' " Galatians 5:13-14 (NKJV)

I felt overwhelming joy that God had heard my prayer to take me but had given me a choice whether to have the surgery or not. At any rate, that was how I interpreted it. I chose to have the surgery because I believed my work on earth was not finished.

After getting a second opinion, I decided on Dr. John Bell at the University of Tennessee (UT) Cancer Center to do the surgery. He was a great fit for me as he not only discussed the lumpectomy procedure he would be doing, but he also drew diagrams on the examining table paper that showed exactly where he would be excising the lump and what the final results would be. Then, he tore the sheet of paper off and handed it to me. Since I like to be knowledgeable and prepared, I went home and studied the map, so to speak. Dr. Bell is a caring, compassionate doctor who takes the time to listen to all of a patient's concerns and provide amply for her needs. I was blessed to have Dr. Bell perform the surgery, and as it turns out, I did not need either chemo or radiation, for which I was extremely grateful.

> ". . . choose for yourselves this day whom you will serve. . . . as for me and my house, we will serve the Lord." Joshua 24:15 (NKJV)

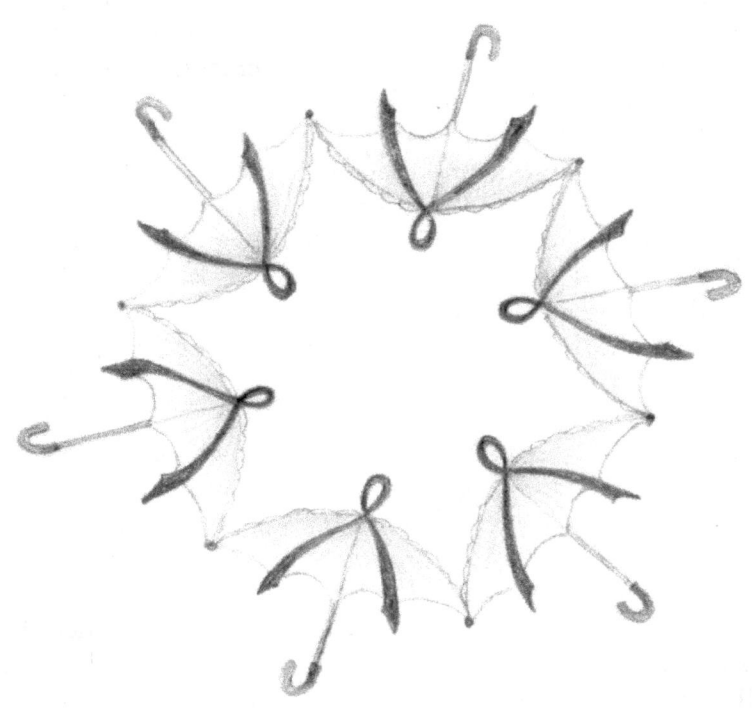

GOD'S WORK

"... through love serve one another ...." Galatians 5:13 (NKJV)

I knew that my work was not yet finished on this plane of existence, but I didn't know exactly what God still wanted me to do. Since my "job" for six years had been taking care of Kevin, I was at a loss of what to do next. Being "retired" from work and caretaking left me with a lot of time on my hands, and because I was a human "doing" instead of a human "being," I had to learn how to just "be." I didn't have to have a life's plan figured out for the next ten years, like I had done in the past. I just had to follow the leading of Spirit one day at a time, and that was mainly to keep putting one foot in front of the other. It was not anything that my ego would call spectacular or publicly noteworthy that would be my calling. Instead, it was to continue to make cards, to see friends on a regular basis, to offer support and encouragement, and to take trips to further my own growth and development.

A few months before I had been diagnosed with breast cancer, I started making cards with my friends Kimberly and Monica and had found a certain satisfaction in doing so. But now I felt led to make specific kinds of cards and little boxes filled with candy that would be relevant for cancer patients and Meals on Wheels recipients, as well as for friends. I remembered when my husband would be in chemo and would find a bit of respite in the cancer center's candy stash. I felt an inner nudge to contribute to their supply with "thinking of you" cards and boxes of sweets.

It was also very important to continue to meet one on one with my friends to lend a listening ear and to offer words of hope and encouragement, when needed. This too, was something I was already doing, but I needed to continue to serve others more in this way.

And lastly, God provided me with a number of trips that I could enjoy and share with my friends. The many varied experiences I had of God's love and kindness on these adventures were continual reminders of His care for our well-being. We are meant to enjoy all of the rich blessings that are offered to us if we but take the risk to get out of our comfort zones and try them. Those trips enriched my life and contributed to my overall spiritual growth and development, enabling me to serve and love others even more each time I returned home.

So, I did not write a great novel, compose a top ten song, or direct the next blockbuster movie, which, at any rate, would all have been ego-driven. Instead, I did try to love others the best I could through God using me as His voice, ears, hands, and feet. My hope is that the following verse can be said of me.

"His lord said to him, 'Well *done*, good and faithful servant; you were faithful over a few things, I will make you ruler over many things. Enter into the joy of your lord.'" Matthew 25:21 (NKJV)

AN EMOTIONAL 24 HOURS

"For this is the message that you heard from the beginning, that we should love one another. . . let us not love in word or in tongue, but in deed and in truth." 1 John 3:11, 18 (NKJV)

I am so blessed to have a cadre of friends who show their love for others by their good works. This morning I had lunch with two such women, Marsha and Terri. Marsha had just returned from a trip to Australia with friend Denise for an Ageless Grace seminar that Denise had designed. I was very impressed that even though Marsha was in a seminar and quite busy that she took the time to bring back a book for me, *The ABC of Compassionate Communication*. What a thoughtful and kind gesture, but then that's who Marsha is. Her intent is to be loving-kindness, and that is who she has become. The week before, Terri made a tasty spaghetti dinner for me, complete with a loaf of sourdough bread. It was all so delicious and exactly what my body was craving. I get teary-eyed thinking about how caring and compassionate these friends are, and I am beyond grateful.

After I left Terri and Marsha, I headed for Lenoir City to see an oral surgeon recommended by my dentist. I had a sore spot on my lower gum and the dentist sent me to have it biopsied. The oral surgeon, Dr. Gross, examined it and said that there was a tiny piece of bone exposed where the skin had been rubbed away. Underneath the bone new skin was trying to break through, but first, the bone had to be flicked off for the area to heal. He very adeptly used an instrument to scrape the tiny bone fragment, and in the blink of an eye it was off. Afterward, we talked about God and the illness that I have and he was very empathetic and attentive.

Dr. Gross wanted to see me back in two weeks to make sure that my gum had properly healed. As he walked me out to the receptionist to make another appointment, he left my folder with her and then returned to his other patients. I pulled my credit card out to pay my bill, but the receptionist would not take it. She said there was no charge for my appointment. I said, "No, that can't be. I know it's supposed to be $93." She said that's just how Dr. Gross was—a kind, caring Christian—and he was not charging me for the visit. I cried again, a second time that day, thanking God for surrounding me with folks who were so loving. I knew beyond a shadow of a doubt that God was showing His great love for me through these fine people.

Yesterday, I saw my surgeon, Dr. Gray, who is also a very caring and compassionate doctor. As soon as he walks into the examining room, I feel this peace that "passes all understanding" descend on me. His nurses tell me that he walks with God every morning before he arrives at the clinic. I believe them! He carefully and patiently listens to all of my questions and thoughtfully answers my concerns. I have the utmost faith and trust in him because I know he talks with God. I ask him to pray with me and he does. I can tell that he has this intimate relationship with a Heavenly Father, one that I desperately want. I only have it part time, but I desire to have it all of the time, which I can tell that Dr. Gray has. He is the finest example of an obedient servant who literally believes in providing the best of care to his patients. I cried in his office and all the way home—tears of joy—thanking God for providing me with such an outstanding surgeon. God is unquestionably showing me time and again His unfathomable love for me by surrounding me with loving souls, and my eyes have been opened to seeing and experiencing their good works. My heart is filled with gratitude!

"Let your light so shine before men, that they may see your good works and glorify your Father in heaven." Matthew 5:16 (NKJV)

THE C-WORD

"Because Your lovingkindness *is* better than life, My lips shall praise
Thus I will bless You while I live." Psalm 63:3-4 (NKJV)

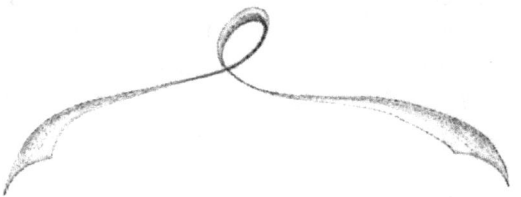

In May I had a colonoscopy which I had hoped would be my last. I had one polyp which turned out to be benign and so it was recommended that my next colonoscopy be in five years, not yearly. Everything went well with the procedure, but a week later I developed a urinary tract infection and was put on antibiotics. The first round did not work, so I was put on a different antibiotic to clear it up. That didn't work, either. I came down with clostridium difficile (C Diff), an intestinal bacteria of the colon, which can be caused by antibiotics that destroy the good bacteria. I was put on three subsequent antibiotics specifically for the C Diff, but none of them cleared it up. It was during this time that I became jaundiced and found myself, once again, in the doctor's office. The lab report stated that my liver enzymes were elevated. Consequently, my physician recommended that an ultrasound and magnetic resonance imaging scan (MRI) be performed to determine the exact cause.

I was referred to my gastroenterologist who put in a stent to clear up the jaundice. He also took a sample of the pancreatic tissue for biopsy. It was shortly afterward that I was diagnosed with stage III pancreatic cancer, the C-Word. I was referred to a pancreatic surgeon and oncologist at UT Hospital Cancer Center in Knoxville. After more tests, it was determined that I would need at least six months of chemo and radiation before I could even be considered for Whipple surgery, which can be a twelve-hour grueling ordeal. I was given a life expectancy of less than one year if I did nothing. With the chemo and radiation I could live one to two years, and if the tumor shrank and I made it to the surgery, I might have three years. But for me, they would be torturous years with all of these things being done to my body. The statistics are grim for the survival rate of pancreatic cancer, less than nine percent, because it is usually caught too late. There is no current test for it and by the time it is found, it is often stage III or stage IV and has spread to other parts of the body, as mine had to a lymph node.

I asked my friends to pray for me to discern God's will because, most importantly, I wanted to know what God wanted me to do. After much prayer and soul searching, I began to believe that God was calling me home this time. When I'd been diagnosed with breast cancer, it was almost a trivial thing, but being diagnosed with pancreatic cancer was huge. It is considered one of the worst cancers to contract and is almost impossible to cure. Because I believe that God does not want us to suffer needlessly, I opted to have no treatment. Since I believe that everything works together for good, I could see how the C Diff was used by God in my decision-making process. I was so sick for months from this illness that I couldn't imagine feeling that way as I underwent any treatment options.

I honestly have felt very blessed throughout this whole process, especially for knowing that my time is limited. For one thing, I needed to create a will which I had been putting off. Also, I felt that God wanted me to publish these essays and try to get them into the hands of people who would benefit from hearing my story. Now, those two things are coming to completion, and I am listening and following that still small voice as God leads me all the way home.

> ". . . Let me die the death of the righteous . . . ."
> Numbers 23:10 (NKJV)

OPTIONS

> ". . . Choose for yourselves this day whom you will serve. . ."
> Joshua 24:15 (NKJV)

This last essay has, for some reason, been the hardest one to write. Macy, Brooke, and I were discussing the book *Option B* by Sheryl Sandberg and Adam Grant, at Panera Bread restaurant recently. I was bemoaning the fact that I still had one more essay to write to complete my book, and I had no idea about what to write. Macy suggested I write about options. What a great topic it is—one that I've had a lot of experience with in this past year as I have tried out different options to soothe and comfort myself while I walked through this time of grief.

When Kevin died, I had no idea how I was going to make it through the year. For a number of months, all I could do was just put one foot in front of the other. But, fortunately, along the way, I noticed I had a treasure trove of options that my Higher Power provided for me to help me cope with the despair, sorrow, and anguish that I felt. Grief support groups, friends, crossword puzzles, card making, meditation, and book clubs were just a few of those options. I still was unable to read all the way to the end of a book, because invariably I would start to obsess about my situation, but I was able to read short articles in magazines and periodicals which was good enough for me.

On this journey, I have found there is no right or wrong way to experience and process grief. Life is a conundrum, an interesting tapestry of joy and sorrow that are intertwined. The more I was able to let my grief out, the more joy I was able to let in and experience. And, I found that I could feel both joy and sorrow at the same time. It wasn't an "either/or" situation, as much as it was an "and/both" experience. My spirit could be joyful, while another part of me was sad. The dichotomy of experiencing opposites was ever present, and I believe God intended for it to be that way. The concept was to embrace diversity rather than try to change the grief into something else.

More than anything else, I had to practice the option of staying in the present moment. If I thought about the past or future, I would often be thrown into a state of angst, fear, and/or overwhelming sadness. When my friend Monica or other folks would ask how I was doing, I tried to respond with how I was in the present moment. That made it more manageable and easier to address. If I really thought about it, I *was* fine in the present moment. It was when I wandered away from the "now" that things were not okay, not fine. I really appreciated the friends who gave me the opportunity to talk about it.

The book *Option B* points to resilience as a necessary trait to possess in order to effectively process painful events. Fortunately for me, Kevin taught me to be resilient. Daily, sometimes hourly, I make the choice to trust my Higher Power to show me the next step forward. As I recognize that painful events are a part of life and aren't personal, pervasive, or permanent (the 3 P's from psychologist Martin Seligman), I am better able to cope and give thanks in all the events that occur in my life, not just what I deem as positive. Through the crack created by my sorrow and loss, I can opt to let all the blessings (treasures) that God intends for me to come into my life.

". . . I will command My blessing on you . . . ." Leviticus 25:21 (NKJV)

ABOUT THE AUTHOR

While struggling to keep both body and soul together during her husband, Kevin's, three year cancer ordeal and its aftermath, Phyllis (Dakota) Evanenko March was led to write about her experiences. Treasures were daily appearing on her horizon. The more she looked, the more gifts she received. Many gems were always there, but it was only when her blinders were removed that she could perceive and appreciate them. This book is about "finding" and "seeing" the treasures that God provides on a daily basis and the inner conviction to write about them. Phyllis lives in Knoxville, Tennessee.

ACKNOWLEDGEMENTS

I would like to recognize the following people who have been with me, in some or many ways, on this arduous journey. I appreciate the cards, flowers, food, phone calls, visits, gifts, coffees, lunches, and dinners, as well as the many other ways that you showed up for me in love and service. To preserve anonymity, last names will not be used. You know who you are and I am greatly indebted to all of you.

Teresa & Dan, Kimberly & Tom, Nancy & Tim, Marsha & Don, Macy & Jim, Kathy & Jim, Terri & Marius, Patricia & Larry, Jay Kay & Matteo, Monica & Don, Lori & Rob, Mitzi & Chuck, Connie & Dick, Brenda, Brooke, Mary, Jeannie, Lyle, Carol, David, Charles, Beth, Caroline, Amy, Anne, Denise, Heather, Joe, Judy, Kelly, Kay, Lana, Patricia, Maureen, Nina, Suzanne, Valerie, Victoria, Inna, and Berniece.

www.ingramcontent.com/pod-product-compliance
Lightning Source LLC
Chambersburg PA
CBHW070614050426
42450CB00011B/3060